What People Are Saying about *Threshold Bible Study*

"To know and love Jesus and to follow him, we need to know and love the sacred Scriptures. For many years now, the *Threshold Bible Study* has proven to be a vital tool for Catholics seeking to go deeper in their encounter with Christ."
ARCHBISHOP JOSÉ H. GOMEZ, *Archbishop of Los Angeles*

"*Threshold Bible Study* offers solid scholarship and spiritual depth. It can be counted on for lively individual study and prayer, even while it offers spiritual riches to deepen communal conversation and reflection among the people of God."
SCOTT HAHN, *Founder and President, St. Paul Center for Biblical Theology*

"Stephen Binz provides the church with a tremendous gift and resource in the *Threshold Bible Study*. This great series invites readers into the world of Scripture with insight, wisdom, and accessibility. This series will help you fall in love with the word of God!"
DANIEL P. HORAN, **OFM**, *Catholic Theological Union, Chicago*

"Stephen J. Binz has a unique talent for helping ordinary folks engage the Bible with deep understanding. Graduates of the Hartford Catholic Biblical School are using his *Threshold Bible Study* throughout Connecticut to bring Scripture more fully into the lives of God's people."
B.J. DALY HORELL, *Director, Catholic Biblical School, Archdiocese of Hartford*

"*Threshold Bible Study* is by far the best series of short Bible study books available today. I recommend them to all the leaders I help train in the Catholic Bible Institutes of several dioceses. Kudos to Stephen Binz for writing books that are ideal for small-group or individual use."
FELIX JUST, **SJ**, *Loyola Marymount University, Los Angeles*

"Stephen Binz's *Threshold Bible Study* series gives adults of all ages a very accessible way to 'open wide the Scriptures' as *Dei Verbum* urged. Encountering the word of God together in study groups will allow participants to deepen their faith and encounter their Savior, Jesus."
ARCHBISHOP JOSEPH E. KURTZ, *Archbishop of Louisville*

"Though the distance many feel between the word of God and their everyday lives can be overwhelming, it need not be so. *Threshold Bible Study* is a fine blend of the best of biblical scholarship and a realistic sensitivity to the spiritual journey of the believing Christian. I recommend it highly."

FRANCIS J. MOLONEY, SDB, *Professor, Catholic University of Australia*

"*Threshold Bible Study* is a refreshing approach to enable participants to ponder the Scriptures more deeply. This series provides a practical way for faithful people to get to know the Bible better and to enjoy the fruits of biblical prayer."

IRENE NOWELL, OSB, *Mount St. Scholastica, Atchison, Kansas*

"*Threshold Bible Study* is appropriately named, for its commentary and study questions bring people to the threshold of the text and invite them in. The questions guide but do not dominate. Stephen Binz's work stands in the tradition of the biblical renewal movement and brings it back to life."

KATHLEEN M. O'CONNOR, *Professor Emerita, Columbia Theological Seminary*

"*Threshold Bible Study* takes to heart the summons of the Second Vatican Council—'easy access to sacred Scripture should be provided for all the Christian faithful' (*Dei Verbum*, 22)—by facilitating an encounter with the word of God that is simple, insightful, and engaging. A great resource for the New Evangelization."

HOSFFMAN OSPINO, *Professor, Boston College School of Theology and Ministry*

"Stephen J. Binz is a consistently outstanding Catholic educator and communicator whose books on the study and application of Scripture have thoroughly enriched my Christian understanding. In our fast-moving, often confusing times, his ability to help us examine and comprehend the truth through all the noise is especially needed and valuable."

ELIZABETH SCALIA, *writer and speaker, editor at Aleteia, blogger as The Anchoress*

"*Threshold Bible Study* helpfully introduces the lay reader into the life-enhancing process of *lectio divina*, individually or in a group. This series leads the reader from Bible study to personal prayer, community involvement, and active Christian commitment in the world."

SANDRA M. SCHNEIDERS, *Professor, Jesuit School of Theology at Santa Clara University*

"Stephen Binz has created an essential resource for the new evangelization rooted in the discipleship process that helps participants to unpack the treasures of the Scriptures in an engaging and accessible manner. *Threshold Bible Study* connects faith learning to faithful living, leading one to a deeper relationship with Christ and his body, the church."

JULIANNE STANZ, *Director of New Evangelization, Diocese of Green Bay*

The Holy Spirit
and
Spiritual Gifts

Stephen J. Binz

TWENTY-THIRD PUBLICATIONS

twentythirdpublications.com

Eighth printing 2019

TWENTY-THIRD PUBLICATIONS
One Montauk Avenue, Suite 200
New London, CT 06320
(860) 437-3012 or (800) 321-0411
www.twentythirdpublications.com

ISBN 978-1-58595-372-1
Library of Congress Catalog Card Number: 2006937353
Printed in the U.S.A.

A division of Bayard, Inc.

Contents

LESSONS 13–18

LESSONS 19–24

LESSONS 25–30

How to Use
Threshold Bible Study

E ach book in the Threshold Bible Study series is designed to lead you through a new doorway of biblical awareness, to accompany you across a unique threshold of understanding. The characters, places, and images that you encounter in each of these topical studies will help you explore fresh dimensions of your faith and discover richer insights for your spiritual life.

Threshold Bible Study covers biblical themes in depth in a short amount of time. Unlike more traditional Bible studies that treat a biblical book or series of books, Threshold Bible Study aims to address specific topics within the entire Bible. The goal is not for you to comprehend everything about each passage, but rather for you to understand what a variety of passages from different books of the Bible reveals about the topic of each study.

Threshold Bible Study offers you an opportunity to explore the entire Bible from the viewpoint of a variety of different themes. The commentary that follows each biblical passage launches your reflection about that passage and helps you begin to see its significance within the context of your contemporary experience. The questions following the commentary challenge you to understand the passage more fully and apply it to your own life. The prayer starter helps conclude your study by integrating learning into your relationship with God.

These studies are designed for maximum flexibility. Each study is presented in a workbook format, with sections for reading, reflecting, writing, discussing, and praying. Space for writing after each question is ideal for personal study and allows group members to prepare in advance for their discussion. The thirty lessons in each topic may be used by an individual over the period of a month, or by a group for six sessions, with lessons to be studied each week before the next group meeting. These studies are ideal for Bible study groups, small Christian communities, adult faith formation, student groups, Sunday school, neighborhood groups, and family reading, as well as for individual learning.

The method of Threshold Bible Study is rooted in the classical tradition of *lectio divina*, an ancient yet contemporary means for reading the Scriptures reflectively and prayerfully. Reading and interpreting the text (*lectio*) is followed by reflective meditation on its message (*meditatio*). This reading and reflecting flows into prayer from the heart (*oratio* and *contemplatio*).

This ancient method assures us that Bible study is a matter of both the mind and the heart. It is not just an intellectual exercise to learn more and be able to discuss the Bible with others. It is, more importantly, a transforming experience. Reflecting on God's word, guided by the Holy Spirit, illumines the mind with wisdom and stirs the heart with zeal.

Following the personal Bible study, Threshold Bible Study offers a method for extending *lectio divina* into a weekly conversation with a small group. This communal experience will allow participants to enhance their appreciation of the message and build up a spiritual community (*collatio*). The end result will be to increase not only individual faith, but also faithful witness in the context of daily life (*operatio*).

Through the spiritual disciplines of Scripture reading, study, reflection, conversation, and prayer, you will experience God's grace more abundantly as your life is rooted more deeply in Christ. The risen Jesus said: "Listen! I am standing at the door, knocking; if you hear my voice and open the door, I will come in to you and eat with you, and you with me" (Rev 3:20). Listen to the word of God, open the door, and cross the threshold to an unimaginable dwelling with God!

SUGGESTIONS FOR INDIVIDUAL STUDY

• Make your Bible reading a time of prayer. Ask for God's guidance as your read the Scriptures.

• Try to study daily, or as often as possible according to the circumstances of your life.

• Read the Bible passage carefully, trying to understand both its meaning and its personal application as you read. Some persons find it helpful to read the passage aloud.

• Read the passage in another Bible translation. Each version adds to your understanding of the original text.

• Allow the commentary to help you comprehend and apply the scriptural text. The commentary is only a beginning, not the last word on the meaning of the passage.

• After reflecting on each question, write out your responses. The very act of writing will help you clarify your thoughts, bring new insights, and amplify your understanding.

• As you reflect on your answers, think about how you can live God's word in the context of your daily life.

• Conclude each daily lesson by reading the prayer and continuing with your own prayer from the heart.

• Make sure your reflections and prayers are matters of both the mind and the heart. A true encounter with God's word is always a transforming experience.

• Choose a word or a phrase from the lesson to carry with you throughout the day as a reminder of your encounter with God's life-changing word.

• Share your learning experience with at least one other person whom you trust for additional insights and affirmation. The ideal way to share learning is in a small group that meets regularly.

SUGGESTIONS FOR GROUP STUDY

• Meet regularly; weekly is ideal. Try to be on time and make attendance a high priority for the sake of the group. The average group meets for about an hour.

• Open each session with a prepared prayer, a song, or a reflection. Find some appropriate way to bring the group from the workaday world into a sacred time of graced sharing.

• If you have not been together before, nametags are very helpful as a group begins to become acquainted with the other group members.

• Spend the first session getting acquainted with one another, reading the Introduction aloud, and discussing the questions that follow.

• Appoint a group facilitator to provide guidance to the discussion. The role of facilitator may rotate among members each week. The facilitator simply keeps the discussion on track; each person shares responsibility for the group. There is no need for the facilitator to be a trained teacher.

• Try to study the six lessons on your own during the week. When you have done your own reflection and written your own answers, you will be better prepared to discuss the six scriptural lessons with the group. If you have not had an opportunity to study the passages during the week, meet with the group anyway to share support and insights.

• Participate in the discussion as much as you are able, offering your thoughts, insights, feelings, and decisions. You learn by sharing with others the fruits of your study.

• Be careful not to dominate the discussion. It is important that everyone in the group be offered an equal opportunity to share the results of their work. Try to link what you say to the comments of others so that the group remains on the topic.

• When discussing your own personal thoughts or feelings, use "I" language. Be as personal and honest as appropriate and be very cautious about giving advice to others.

• Listen attentively to the other members of the group so as to learn from their insights. The words of the Bible affect each person in a different way, so a group provides a wealth of understanding for each member.

• Don't fear silence. Silence in a group is as important as silence in personal study. It allows individuals time to listen to the voice of God's Spirit and the opportunity to form their thoughts before they speak.

• Solicit several responses for each question. The thoughts of different people will build on the answers of others and will lead to deeper insights for all.

• Don't fear controversy. Differences of opinions are a sign of a healthy and honest group. If you cannot resolve an issue, continue on, agreeing to disagree. There is probably some truth in each viewpoint.

• Discuss the questions that seem most important for the group. There is no need to cover all the questions in the group session.

• Realize that some questions about the Bible cannot be resolved, even by experts. Don't get stuck on some issue for which there are no clear answers.

• Whatever is said in the group is said in confidence and should be regarded as such.

• Pray as a group in whatever way feels comfortable. Pray for the members of your group throughout the week.

Schedule for group study

Session 1: Introduction   Date: _____

Session 2: Lessons 1–6   Date: _____

Session 3: Lessons 7–12   Date: _____

Session 4: Lessons 13–18   Date: _____

Session 5: Lessons 19–24   Date: _____

Session 6: Lessons 25–30   Date: _____

God's love has been poured into our hearts through the Holy Spirit that has been given to us. Rom 5:5

The Holy Spirit and Spiritual Gifts

The heart of the spiritual life is the realization that God is always present. This divine presence is revealed to us through creation and through sacred Scripture. As we observe God's world and as we read the inspired Scriptures, we perceive God's animating presence more and more, until we can say with the psalmist, "Where can I go from your spirit? Or where can I flee from your presence?" (Ps 139:7).

The Holy Spirit works invisibly within us, always making God's outward revelation inward in us. God's Spirit works in our minds, giving knowledge, and in our hearts, giving love. These two complementary and inseparable ways that the Spirit is manifested to us correspond to the two great pronouncements about God's inner nature in John's letters: "God is light" (1 John 1:5) and "God is love" (1 John 4:8). As a shining light, the Spirit leads disciples to the fullness of truth, overcoming ignorance and offering understanding of God's revelation. As fervent love, the Spirit guides disciples to an intimate relationship with God, conquering our greed and fostering generosity and compassion.

The Holy Spirit works within us to make us see God in a new way—not as a taskmaster who impedes our freedom, but as the personal source of our deepest joy. As a new relationship with God is formed within us, the Holy

Spirit teaches us two pivotal realities in the depths of our hearts: to speak to God as Abba, Father, and to know Jesus as Kyrios, Lord.

What God's Spirit did in the life of Jesus—giving him the experience of his own relationship as Son to the Father and moving him in the depths of his heart to cry "Abba!"—the Spirit continues in us. In the Holy Spirit, we realize that the transcendent Creator of the world is an intimate parent to us. By pouring the love of God into our hearts, the Holy Spirit makes known the Father's love within us. As Paul tells us, "God has sent the Spirit of his Son into our hearts, crying, 'Abba! Father!'" (Gal 4:6). The Spirit gives us not just an abstract knowledge of God's love, but the interior experience of God's personal and intense love for us.

The Holy Spirit also brings us to an interior awareness that Jesus Christ is risen and alive. When the Spirit descended upon the church at Pentecost, the meaning of Christ's life became clear to the disciples, and Peter was able to proclaim him as "both Lord and Messiah" (Acts 2:36). God's Spirit does the same for us, enlightening us within and bearing witness to the full revelation of God in Christ. In the words of Paul, "No one can say 'Jesus is Lord' except by the Holy Spirit" (1 Cor 12:3).

Reflection and discussion

• What do I already know about the nature of the Holy Spirit?

• What does it mean to me to call God "Abba" and to call Jesus "Lord"?

Natural Symbols of the Spirit: Wind, Water, Fire, and Oil

The biblical name for Spirit in Hebrew is *ruach*, a word which can mean either wind or breath, in addition to Spirit. The Greek word, *pneuma*, and the Latin word, *spiritus*, also express the multiple senses of wind, breath, and Spirit.

The wind is a sweeping force that cannot be contained, and thus, the image of the wind expresses the power, freedom, and transcendence of God's Spirit. Breath, on the other hand, is what is most intimate, inward, and personal, so the image of breath conveys the gentleness, peacefulness, and immanence of the Spirit. In the Acts of the Apostles, the Spirit is manifested at Pentecost with a strong, rushing wind (2:2). In John's gospel, Jesus breathes on his disciples and says, "Receive the Holy Spirit" (20:22). The Holy Spirit personifies this mystery of God's presence, which is both awesome power and overwhelming tenderness, a divine presence that inspires in people both reverent fear and irresistible attraction.

Since water is so closely associated with life and renewal, it has become in the Scriptures a sacramental expression of God's Spirit. God promises to pour out his Spirit as he pours water on thirsty land (Isa 44:3). Jesus referred to the Spirit as a river of living water which believers would receive (John 7:38–39). When the desert of our soul cries out to God, he pours out the refreshing Spirit of new life. Jesus described entry into God's kingdom as "being born of water and Spirit" (John 3:5). In the early church, the waters of baptism expressed the grace of the Holy Spirit bringing a believer into the Christian life.

Fire is another natural element that becomes a scriptural symbol for God's Spirit. John the Baptist proclaimed that Jesus would baptize "with the Holy Spirit and fire" (Matt 3:11). Luke reported that tongues of fire rested on the disciples at Pentecost as they were filled with the Holy Spirit (Acts 2:3–4). Only what is precious is tested by fire to purify it, gold among material things and faith among spiritual realities (1 Pet 1:7). God's fiery Spirit destroys our impurity and cleanses us through and through, making us shine like gold. Then after accomplishing its purifying effect, the fire of the Spirit warms us with God's affection and sets us aflame with fervor. The radical change experienced by the fearful disciples when they received the Holy Spirit demonstrates the transforming effects of the Spirit's fire. The remedy for lukewarm, apathetic Christianity is the gift of the Holy Spirit. The flame of the Spirit enlightens our minds with wisdom and enkindles our hearts with zeal.

Olive oil scented with perfume became the sacred chrism by which the priests, kings, and prophets of Israel were anointed. This anointing with oil conferred an inner power and transformation that became increasingly associated with God's Spirit. This link between anointing and the Spirit is exemplified in the text of Isaiah: "The spirit of the Lord God is upon me, because the Lord has anointed me" (61:1). At his baptism, Jesus was anointed with the Holy Spirit as the long-awaited messianic priest, prophet, and king. As the Christ, the Anointed One, Jesus' entire ministry was lived in the Spirit until he poured out that Spirit upon the church through his death and resurrection. Now, through the Spirit of the risen Christ, the church is the body of Christ, and all the people of God are anointed in the Holy Spirit by faith and baptism. From this baptismal anointing in the Spirit we are made Christians and partake in Christ's messianic work in the world.

Reflection and discussion

• Why does God choose to reveal the Spirit's presence and power through the natural elements of the created world? Through what natural symbol do I most experience the Holy Spirit?

It is easier to understand the power & nature of Jesus thru symbolism

• In what way does the Hebrew meaning of Spirit convey two different but complementary aspects of the Spirit's presence?

Hebrew meaning ruah of spirit aswell wind or breath
wind expressing power & strength of God
breath gentleness ever subtle presence

The Spirit's Work from Creation to New Creation

This study of the Holy Spirit will examine four different sections of the biblical literature. First, we will look at God's Spirit in the Old Testament. We will then see the way that three different New Testament writers—Luke, John, and Paul—express the work of the Holy Spirit and the Spirit's many gifts.

The Spirit is first manifested in the Bible as God's creative presence, the wind sweeping over the chaotic waters at creation (Gen 1:2) and the divine breath which animates the creation of humanity (Gen 2:7). As the Spirit is revealed through the prophets, God's Spirit is described as that divine presence which continually enlivens and renews creation, bringing all things eventually to their perfection. The Holy Spirit is not confined to God's revelation in Israel or even the church, but the Spirit's sphere of activity is as wide as creation itself: "The spirit of the Lord has filled the world" (Wis 1:7). Wherever people search for truth, goodness, and beauty, God's Spirit is the source of that pursuit. Thomas Aquinas said, "Every truth, no matter what its source is said to be, comes from the Holy Spirit." In the hearts of all people, the Holy Spirit works to bring people to ask the basic questions that stimulate the human quest for God.

Luke begins his gospel by announcing that God's Son would be conceived in the womb of Mary through the power of the Holy Spirit. Through this universal Spirit, Jesus would be not only the Messiah of Israel but the Savior of the world. As he begins the Acts of the Apostles, Luke announces the descent of the Holy Spirit upon the church gathered in Jerusalem. This outpouring of God's Spirit not only fulfills God's promises to Israel, but initiates the universal work of the new creation. The Spirit that filled Jesus throughout his earthly ministry is unleashed upon the newborn church in wind and fire, animating its witness "to the ends of the earth" (Acts 1:8).

In John's gospel, the Spirit is called the Paraclete, or Advocate, and is the continuing presence of the glorified Jesus in his disciples. In one amazing passage, Jesus declares, "It is to your advantage that I go away, for if I do not go away, the Advocate will not come to you" (John 16:7). In the Holy Spirit, God's presence is not limited to any one time or place, as it was in the bodily presence of Jesus. Through the Spirit, the glorified Jesus is present to every time and culture, just as present today as in the lives of his first disciples. The Paraclete is also called "the Spirit of truth," who will guide the church through the ages "into all the truth" (John 16:13). Because there were many things that the disciples could not understand during the earthly life of Jesus, the Spirit would provide new insights and guidance for the church in every time and culture. Only the post-resurrection gift of the Holy Spirit taught the disciples the full meaning of what they had seen and heard in Jesus, and the Spirit empowered them to be witnesses by speaking through them.

The letters of Paul contain numerous insights into the work of the Holy Spirit in the church and in the lives of disciples. The love of God has been poured into our hearts through the Holy Spirit, and we are adopted into the family of God. The Christian life is "life in the Spirit," which is a foretaste of the fullness of life that awaits us. The Spirit intercedes for us, even praying within us, and gives us a desire to praise God. As we live in the Spirit, our lives are filled with the characteristics of divine life: faithfulness, generosity, peace, joy, and especially love. Paul's writings show how the Holy Spirit bestows a variety of spiritual gifts upon the church. Each member of the church is given unique and diverse gifts for the service of others and for the good of the church. The Spirit offers these gifts of divine grace and coordinates them so that they work together in harmony. Like the many different instruments in an orchestra that contribute their own part to the symphony, the spiritual gifts of each member play their part in the movement and harmony of the whole. Together, the Spirit's gifts contribute to the church's glorious masterpiece of praise to God.

Reflection and discussion

• What expresses for me the universality of God's Spirit? What indicates that the Holy Spirit works through human expressions of religion, science, art, and music?

Human nature is the same all over world. We search for meaning Appreciate beauty in nature - It relaxes you & you feel peaceful

• What are the similarities and difference between personal talents and gifts of the Spirit? In what way do these sometimes work together in my life? –

gifts of HS are intuitive & insight

personal talent you must continue to work on just as you must continue to work on relationship with God

The Inspiration of the Holy Spirit

God is revealed to us through created things and inspired words. These two "books" of revelation, the creation that we see and the Scriptures that we read, make God known through the work of the Holy Spirit in us. The wonder of creation becomes a kind of universal sacrament, revealing the wonder of God and leading us to God's life, when we look upon it with the guidance of the Spirit. The Bible reveals the love of God and God's desire to share divine life with us when we read and understand under the direction of the Spirit.

Reading the Bible without the Holy Spirit is like opening a book in the dark. The same Spirit, who inspired the authors of the Scriptures, guides us as we read and reflect upon the biblical passages. When we pray to the Holy Spirit before reading Scripture and read in an atmosphere of trusting faith, the sacred text can come alive with freshness and personal significance. The same Spirit, who comes upon the created gifts of bread and wine so that they become for us the living Christ, hovers over the biblical texts so that they become the living word of God.

Reflection and discussion

• When have I experienced the Spirit's work in revealing God to me through creation or Scripture?

beauty of birth
teaching Kdg and innocense
& kidness of 5 yr olds no filter

• In what way do I want the Holy Spirit to work in my life as I study this work?

Prayer

Spirit of the living God, fall afresh on me. Melt me, mold me, fill me, and use me. I want to understand your energizing presence and open my life more fully to your power. Stir up within me the grace of my baptism in Christ and animate your gifts within me for the service of God's people. Enlighten and encourage me as I read and contemplate your inspired word in these sacred Scriptures. Show me how to make my life a testimony to God's love.

SUGGESTIONS FOR FACILITATORS, GROUP SESSION 1

1. If the group is meeting for the first time, or if there are newcomers joining the group, it is helpful to provide nametags.

2. Distribute the books to the members of the group.

3. You may want to ask the participants to introduce themselves and tell the group a bit about themselves.

4. Ask one or more of these introductory questions:
   - What drew you to join this group?
   - What is your biggest fear in beginning this Bible study?
   - How is beginning this study like a "threshold" for you?

5. You may want to pray this prayer as a group:

Come upon us, Holy Spirit, to enlighten and guide us as we begin this study. You inspired the writers of the Scriptures to reveal your presence throughout the history of salvation. This inspired word has the power to convert our hearts and change our lives. Fill our hearts with desire, trust, and confidence as you shine the light of your truth within us. Motivate us to read the Scriptures and give us a deeper love for God's word each day. Bless us during this session and throughout the coming week with the fire of your love.

6. Read the Introduction aloud, pausing at each question for discussion. Group members may wish to write the insights of the group as each question is discussed. Encourage several members of the group to respond to each question.

7. Don't feel compelled to finish the complete Introduction during the session. It is better to allow sufficient time to talk about the questions raised than to rush to the end. Group members may read any remaining sections on their own after the group meeting.

8. Instruct group members to read the first six lessons on their own during the six days before the next group meeting. They should write out their own answers to the questions as preparation for next week's group discussion.

9. Fill in the date for each group meeting under "Schedule for Group Study."

10. Conclude by praying aloud together the prayer at the end of the Introduction.

The earth was a formless void and darkness covered the face of the deep, while a wind from God swept over the face of the waters. Gen 1:2

Come, Creator Spirit

GENESIS 1:1–3; 2:4–7 ¹*In the beginning when God created the heavens and the earth, ²the earth was a formless void and darkness covered the face of the deep, while a wind from God swept over the face of the waters. ³Then God said, "Let there be light"; and there was light.*

2 ⁴In the day that the Lord God made the earth and the heavens, ⁵when no plant of the field was yet in the earth and no herb of the field had yet sprung up—for the Lord God had not caused it to rain upon the earth, and there was no one to till the ground; ⁶but a stream would rise from the earth, and water the whole face of the ground— ⁷then the Lord God formed man from the dust of the ground, and breathed into his nostrils the breath of life; and the man became a living being.

The Spirit of God is first associated in Scripture with God's work of creation. The creation accounts, which begin the book of Genesis, demonstrate the close connection between divine Spirit, wind, and breath. The description of God's creative presence before creation can be literally translated, "a wind from God swept over the face of the waters" (1:2), as our translation offers, or "the Spirit of God hovered over the waters," as in other translations. The words describing God's creation of the man from the dust of the ground can be translated "God breathed into his nostrils the breath of life" (2:7), or the same Hebrew words can be translated, "God breathed into his nostrils the spirit of life." The image of the wind expresses the force, freedom, and transcenence of God's Spirit; the breath conveys the gentleness, docility, and immanence of that same divine Spirit.

God's Spirit has been engaged in all of God's works from the beginning. Later biblical writers reflect on the personal presence of the divine Spirit in the work of creation. Psalm 104 records: "When you take away their breath (*ruach*), they die and return to their dust. When you send forth your spirit (*ruach*), they are created" (verses 29–30). The psalmist is deliberately echoing the spirit in Genesis 1:2 and 2:7. Likewise, Job proclaims, "The spirit of God has made me, and the breath of the Almighty gives me life" (33:4), again an echo of Genesis 1:2 and 2:7.

God creates through his word and in the power of his Spirit. The divine word is spoken, "let there be…," and the energizing Spirit empowers the word, bringing into being what God speaks. As the psalmist sang: "By the word of the Lord the heavens were made, and all their hosts by the breath (*ruach*) of his mouth" (33:6). Just as the wind makes plants fertile, carrying pollen to make seeds ripen and scattering seeds to the ground to make them germinate, so does the Holy Spirit for the seed that is the word of God. This relationship between God's word and God's Spirit continues in the prophetic literature in which God spoke his word through the prophets by the inspiration of God's Spirit. This anticipates the New Testament understanding that through the word of God, his only Son, all things were made, and in the power of the Holy Spirit, the ongoing work of renewing creation continues.

In describing God's work of creating "the heavens and the earth" (1:1), the author of Genesis shows that God transformed chaos into cosmos, formless void into created order (1:2). Yet, God did not eliminate the two major elements of chaos: darkness and the deep sea. The elements of chaos will continue to move in and out of creation, through storms, destruction, pestilence, and death, until God creates "new heavens and a new earth" (Isa 65:17; Rev 21:1), when all creation will be complete. God is always creating, bringing meaningless chaos into harmonious order, communicating being and energy, continually enlivening and making creation new. The Holy Spirit is the divine energy that renews and perfects creation, the personal power who is always at work bringing creation to its fulfillment, creating and renewing the face of the earth.

What God's Spirit continually does for the cosmos, God does in microcosm for each of us each day. Upon awakening in the morning, we move from the darkness and chaotic confusion of the unconscious to the newly created order of a new day. The creative Spirit is always at work within us, establishing from the abyss of our hearts and souls something more harmonious and bright. That is why the best beginning of each new day is a prayer to the Holy Spirit, a prayer to hover over our chaos and create us anew, until we are fully formed into the glorious creatures we were made to be.

Reflection and discussion

• In what ways do the images of wind and breath express two different dimensions of the work of God's Spirit in the world?

force and gentleness

• In what way do I experience the transcendence and the immanence of God, as represented by the images of divine wind and breath? How can I be attracted both by God's terrifying power and God's irresistible tenderness?

we wake up each morning from darkness and move into the order of the new day

• What is the relationship between God's word and God's Spirit in my understanding of the Bible?

The divine word is spoken and the spirit empowers the word bringing into Being what God speaks

• In what ways will chaos continue to move in and out of creation until the world is perfected by the Holy Spirit?

in the now and the not yet - sin and goodness ebbs & flows

• What is the chaos of the world over which I pray today? What is the chaos within my own heart that I pray God's Spirit bring to order and harmony?

Prayer

Come, Creator Spirit. You who hovered over the darkness of chaos as creation began, come into our world anew. Take this dusty clay of the earth and breathe divine life in me. Transform my darkness into the light of truth and love.

Would that all the Lord's people were prophets,
and that the Lord would put his spirit on them! Num 11:29

The Spirit Rested upon Them

NUMBERS 11:16–30 ¹⁶*So the Lord said to Moses, "Gather for me seventy of the elders of Israel, whom you know to be the elders of the people and officers over them; bring them to the tent of meeting, and have them take their place there with you.* ¹⁷*I will come down and talk with you there; and I will take some of the spirit that is on you and put it on them; and they shall bear the burden of the people along with you so that you will not bear it all by yourself.* ¹⁸*And say to the people: Consecrate yourselves for tomorrow, and you shall eat meat; for you have wailed in the hearing of the Lord, saying, 'If only we had meat to eat! Surely it was better for us in Egypt.' Therefore the Lord will give you meat, and you shall eat.* ¹⁹*You shall eat not only one day, or two days, or five days, or ten days, or twenty days,* ²⁰*but for a whole month—until it comes out of your nostrils and becomes loathsome to you—because you have rejected the Lord who is among you, and have wailed before him, saying, 'Why did we ever leave Egypt?'"* ²¹*But Moses said, "The people I am with number six hundred thousand on foot; and you say, 'I will give them meat, that they may eat for a whole month'!* ²²*Are there enough flocks and herds to slaughter for them? Are there enough fish in the sea to catch for them?"* ²³*The Lord said to Moses, "Is the Lord's power limited? Now you shall see whether my word will come true for you or not."*

^{24}*So Moses went out and told the people the words of the Lord; and he gathered seventy elders of the people, and placed them all around the tent.* ^{25}*Then the Lord came down in the cloud and spoke to him, and took some of the spirit that was on him and put it on the seventy elders; and when the spirit rested upon them, they prophesied. But they did not do so again.*

^{26}*Two men remained in the camp, one named Eldad, and the other named Medad, and the spirit rested on them; they were among those registered, but they had not gone out to the tent, and so they prophesied in the camp.* ^{27}*And a young man ran and told Moses, "Eldad and Medad are prophesying in the camp."* ^{28}*And Joshua son of Nun, the assistant of Moses, one of his chosen men, said, "My lord Moses, stop them!"* ^{29}*But Moses said to him, "Are you jealous for my sake? Would that all the Lord's people were prophets, and that the Lord would put his spirit on them!"* ^{30}*And Moses and the elders of Israel returned to the camp.*

Though God had given Moses the gift of his divine Spirit to enable him to govern the Hebrew people as they came out of Egypt on their journey to the promised land, Moses faced rebellion and turmoil among the people. Dissatisfied with God's gift of a daily diet of manna during their desert trek, the people were demanding meat to eat and threatening to return to Egypt. But God told Moses to gather seventy of Israel's elders and bring them to the tabernacle of God's presence. There, God would disperse the Spirit he had given to Moses and place the Spirit on the seventy elders so that they would share in the burden of ruling God's redeemed people (verse 17). Just as the Spirit produced order and purpose out of the formless chaos in Genesis 1, so here God's Spirit worked creatively to produce communal and religious order in the midst of the social chaos of God's newborn people.

The transmission of God's Spirit to the seventy elders took place at the tent of meeting, the place where God periodically came down in a cloud and spoke with Moses. This installation of the elders to official roles of leadership among God's people took place at the divinely chosen place, and the transfer of the Spirit was enacted by God, whose presence was symbolized by the cloud (verse 25). This new role of ministry among the people derived from the central spiritual gift of Moses and expanded the community's leadership structures. This event of the exodus is comparable to the gospel account in which Jesus appointed seventy and sent them out to share in his mission of teaching and healing. Upon their return from their mission, Jesus rejoiced in the Holy Spirit at all that the seventy had been able to do in his name (Luke 10:1–22).

Two members of the community of Israel, Eldad and Medad, also received the Spirit, enabling them to prophesy, although they were not present during the official installation of the others. Apparently, these two remained in the camp and did not go out to the tent of meeting; thus the Spirit was not conferred through the institutionally recognized channels, but spilled over onto them for the work of prophecy. When Joshua asked that Moses refrain these men from prophesying among the people, Moses responded in a way that expresses the expansive quality of his leadership: "Would that all the Lord's people were prophets, and that the Lord would put his spirit on them!" (verse 29).

Moses welcomed the assistance from the seventy appointed elders, but he also recognized the importance of the inspired voices outside the institutional leadership of God's people. Throughout Israel's history, the words of the prophets regularly challenged kings, judges, and priests who misused their power and led God's people astray. Prophetic voices, like those of Amos and Jeremiah, continued to speak from among God's people, offering inspired words of judgment and hope as the Spirit led them. In every age, God's Spirit speaks in unpredictable ways from outside institutional structures, and God's church must listen and discern the Spirit's voice.

Most significantly, the words of Moses anticipate the universally widespread coming of the Spirit on God's people anticipated for later times. The activity of God's Spirit within God's covenant from Sinai was sporadic and selective. By contrast, the Spirit anticipated in the new covenant would be poured out in unrestrained measure, dwelling personally and permanently within God's people (Joel 2:28–29). What Moses longed for—that God would put his Spirit upon all the people—would become a reality.

Reflection and discussion

• In what way does the work of God's Spirit in creation compare to the Spirit's work in social and religious institutions?

order out of chaos

• How is the work of the Spirit different in the seventy elders than in Eldad and Medad? Why are both legitimate manifestations of the Spirit's work?

they were not in tent where Jesus when spirit rested on everyone - but the had the right spirit in their heart

• What does this episode from Israel's formative period teach God's people today about the work of the Spirit?

That God's spirit rests on everyone. The church is a community where everyone works together

• Do I pray to the Holy Spirit when I feel overwhelmed and am burdened by responsibilities? How can I expect the Spirit to help me?

Yes - Hopefully calms me down and accept what happens

Prayer

Come, Holy Spirit, move within me as you worked in the lives of Moses and the leaders of Israel. Stir up the gift of prophecy within your church and inspire us to be responsible and enthusiastic ministers of your people.

The spirit of the Lord shall rest on him,
the spirit of wisdom and understanding, the spirit of counsel and might,
the spirit of knowledge and the fear of the Lord. Isa 11:2

Gifts of the Spirit for God's Messiah

ISAIAH 11:1–9

A shoot shall come out from the stock of Jesse,
and a branch shall grow out of his roots.
[2]*The spirit of the Lord shall rest on him,*
the spirit of wisdom and understanding,
the spirit of counsel and might,
the spirit of knowledge and the fear of the Lord.
[3]*His delight shall be in the fear of the Lord.*

He shall not judge by what his eyes see,
or decide by what his ears hear;
[4]*but with righteousness he shall judge the poor,*
and decide with equity for the meek of the earth;
he shall strike the earth with the rod of his mouth,
and with the breath of his lips he shall kill the wicked.
[5]*Righteousness shall be the belt around his waist,*
and faithfulness the belt around his loins.

⁶The wolf shall live with the lamb,
    the leopard shall lie down with the kid,
the calf and the lion and the fatling together,
    and a little child shall lead them.
⁷The cow and the bear shall graze,
    their young shall lie down together;
    and the lion shall eat straw like the ox.
⁸The nursing child shall play over the hole of the asp,
    and the weaned child shall put its hand on the adder's den.
⁹They will not hurt or destroy
    on all my holy mountain;
for the earth will be full of the knowledge of the Lord
    as the waters cover the sea.

Isaiah's prophetic text speaks of Israel's ideal future king. He would come from the dynasty of King David, which had been chopped down. From the stump and roots of Jesse (verse 1), the father of David, a new shoot would grow—the Messiah of Israel, a king filled with God's own Spirit. His reign would be an era of peace and justice, and all the nations would look to him.

The Messiah would be anointed not only with oil, but with God's Spirit—the Spirit that would bestow upon him the character necessary to rule justly (verse 2). These gifts of the Spirit belong, first of all, to God, but they are bestowed as gifts upon God's chosen king. This future king would be far more righteous and faithful than King David or any of the other previous monarchs descended from David. He would render good judgments, speak the truth, and protect the rights of the poor because he would be led with God's own Spirit.

The fourfold repetition of "spirit" in verse 2 is striking. The Messiah will be endowed with God's Spirit and all the spiritual gifts necessary for his reign. The Greek translation of Isaiah, used by the early Christians, lists seven gifts, including piety and fear of the Lord as two separate gifts. These seven gifts, belonging first to Christ, are the permanent gifts conferred by God to those baptized and confirmed in the Christian way of life. These seven differ from the more specific gifts of the Spirit—like leadership, prophecy, healing, and discernment—which are selectively given to individuals for the good of the whole community. These seven are freely offered to everyone by God's grace and may be claimed for the building up of God's kingdom.

Isaiah looked to the future for the fulfillment of the hopes dashed in his own day. His words gave voice to Israel's hopes for a new king, a new kingdom. They stood as a trusting promise of the salvation to come. The new king would establish an idyllic kingdom. The images of wild animals dwelling together with their prey—the wolf with the lamb, the leopard with the kid, the lion with the calf, the bear with the cow, the venomous snake and the infant—express the harmony and peace expected for the messianic age (verses 6–8).

The work of God's Spirit, through the coming of God's Messiah, would reverse the world as it had come to be known. War and destruction, so much a part of the experience of Israel through the centuries, would end, and the whole earth would know God (verse 9). Isaiah envisions an earth in which everything is reversed from the violence and degradation it had come to know. This is not a world turned upside down; rather a cosmos turned right side up—God's original intent for creation.

Reflection and discussion

• To whom were the gifts of the Spirit intended? How can they be claimed by all of God's people? *Jesus first now. everyone - spreading word of God and performing acts of mercy*

• In what ways does Isaiah's description of God's messianic kingdom compare to God's original design for creation? What is the role of the Spirit in both?

to be God's presence when he is no longer around

• In what ways is Isaiah's description of God's messianic kingdom fulfilled in the work of Jesus?

Because Jesus was righteousness and non-judgemental

• How are these gifts of the Spirit manifested in pastoral leadership today? Which gift is most essential for leading God's people?

by the various organization elderly Bible study feed the poor

righteousness & counsel

• Which of these gifts of the Spirit do I want God to stir up in me? How can I take hold of that spiritual gift today?

Wisdom - think & wait with decision making

Piety - pray for faith

Prayer

Come, Holy Spirit, let me claim your seven-fold gifts: the gifts of wisdom, understanding, counsel, fortitude, knowledge, piety, and fear of the Lord. Help me use your gifts for God's glory and for building up God's kingdom.

The spirit of the Lord God is upon me, because the Lord has anointed me;
he has sent me to bring good news to the oppressed,
to bind up the broken-hearted, to proclaim liberty to the captives,
and release to the prisoners. Isa 61:1

Anointed with God's Spirit

ISAIAH 42:1–9

Here is my servant, whom I uphold,
my chosen, in whom my soul delights;
I have put my spirit upon him;
he will bring forth justice to the nations.
²He will not cry or lift up his voice,
or make it heard in the street;
³a bruised reed he will not break,
and a dimly burning wick he will not quench;
he will faithfully bring forth justice.
⁴He will not grow faint or be crushed
until he has established justice in the earth;
and the coastlands wait for his teaching.

⁵Thus says God, the Lord,
who created the heavens and stretched them out,
who spread out the earth and what comes from it,
who gives breath to the people upon it

and spirit to those who walk in it:
[6]I am the Lord, I have called you in righteousness,
*   I have taken you by the hand and kept you;*
I have given you as a covenant to the people,
*   a light to the nations,*
[7]to open the eyes that are blind,
to bring out the prisoners from the dungeon,
*   from the prison those who sit in darkness.*
[8]I am the Lord, that is my name;
*   my glory I give to no other,*
*   nor my praise to idols.*
[9]See, the former things have come to pass,
*   and new things I now declare;*
before they spring forth,
*   I tell you of them.*

ISAIAH 61:1–4

The spirit of the Lord God is upon me,
*   because the Lord has anointed me;*
he has sent me to bring good news to the oppressed,
*   to bind up the broken-hearted,*
to proclaim liberty to the captives,
*   and release to the prisoners;*
[2]to proclaim the year of the Lord's favor,
*   and the day of vengeance of our God;*
*   to comfort all who mourn;*
[3]to provide for those who mourn in Zion—
*   to give them a garland instead of ashes,*
the oil of gladness instead of mourning,
*   the mantle of praise instead of a faint spirit.*
They will be called oaks of righteousness,
*   the planting of the Lord, to display his glory.*
[4]They shall build up the ancient ruins,
*   they shall raise up the former devastations;*
they shall repair the ruined cities,
*   the devastations of many generations.*

These two Isaian passages praise the identity and the task of the Servant of the Lord. Much scholarly debate has centered upon whether the Servant is an individual person or the community of God's people personified. But this ambiguity is most probably intentional, so that the Servant was set forth as a model for both the individual and the community who respond to God's call to be his servants in the world. It is the highest ideal for those who accept the call to be agents of God's compassionate reign. In the first hymn (Isa 42), the Servant is introduced and spoken about by God; in the second (Isa 61), the Servant speaks in the first person.

God is the origin of all that the Servant is and is called to do. God presents the Servant, "Here is my servant" (42:1), and identifies himself as the source of the Servant's strength. The terms of introduction are intimate: God has "chosen" the Servant because God "delights" in him. Most importantly, the Servant is anointed and empowered by the Spirit of God: "The Spirit of the Lord God is upon me, because the Lord has anointed me" (61:1). Throughout the Old Testament, weak and ordinary human beings, like prophets, judges, and kings, rise up to accomplish daunting tasks through the empowerment of God's Spirit. As a representational figure of the ideal individual and the community of God, the Servant is anointed by the Spirit to accomplish the divinely appointed work.

The task to which the Servant is called is emphatically set forth: "He will bring forth justice to the nations…establish justice in the earth" (42:1, 4). Justice, in the literature of Israel, is the moral foundation upon which all reality rests. It extends to all nations and even to the natural world. The work of the Servant is to bear witness to God's justice in the world, to be an instrument for bringing justice to God's creation. But the manner in which God's Servant carries out the task of justice stands in stark contrast to the ways of the nations and their leaders. God's justice will be brought to the world by renouncing force, accepting submission, and caring for the wounded (42:2–3; 61:1). The Servant is not a conqueror, but a victim. By embodying God's own patience and compassion, the Servant becomes an instrument of healing and reconciliation.

The gospels demonstrate that both of these Servant hymns were most completely fulfilled in the ministry of Jesus Christ (Matt 12:17–21; Luke 4:16–21). In the life of Jesus, the word of God and the Spirit of God together produce an assurance of his own identity and ministry as God's Messiah. He is the one anointed by God's Spirit, par excellence. He is the model and inspiration for all called by the God of heaven and earth to bring justice to the world. From the one on whom the Spirit rested, we are given that same Spirit to participate in that same mission.

Reflection and discussion

• What are some of the characteristics, according to Isaiah, of being a servant of God?

Righteous
fair / justice
humility

• How do these two hymns of Isaiah direct me in my desire to be a Spirit-led servant of the Lord? What characteristic must I practice more?

By trying to imitate Jesus
practice faith & humility

• In what ways have these hymns been fulfilled completely and perfectly only in Jesus Christ?

Justice to Israel
spirit was always w/ Jesus
Jesus had compassion & understanding

Prayer

Come, Holy Spirit, empower me to respond to God's call to be his servant in the world. Teach me how to be an instrument of liberation, healing, and justice in the place where I live. But keep me unassuming and show me how to respond to God's delight in me.

**Where is the one who put within them his holy spirit,
who caused his glorious arm to march at the right hand of Moses,
who divided the waters before them to make for himself
an everlasting name?** Isa 63:11–12

God's Holy Spirit Redeems Israel

ISAIAH 63:7–14

⁷I will recount the gracious deeds of the Lord,
   the praiseworthy acts of the Lord,
because of all that the Lord has done for us,
   and the great favor to the house of Israel
that he has shown them according to his mercy,
   according to the abundance of his steadfast love.
⁸For he said, "Surely they are my people,
   children who will not deal falsely";
and he became their savior
   ⁹in all their distress.
It was no messenger or angel
   but his presence that saved them;
in his love and in his pity he redeemed them;
   he lifted them up and carried them all the days of old.

¹⁰*But they rebelled*
   and grieved his holy spirit;
therefore he became their enemy;
   he himself fought against them.
¹¹*Then they remembered the days of old,*
   of Moses his servant.
Where is the one who brought them up out of the sea
   with the shepherds of his flock?
Where is the one who put within them
   his holy spirit,
¹²*who caused his glorious arm*
   to march at the right hand of Moses,
who divided the waters before them
   to make for himself an everlasting name,
      ¹³*who led them through the depths?*
Like a horse in the desert,
   they did not stumble.
¹⁴*Like cattle that go down into the valley,*
   the spirit of the Lord gave them rest.
Thus you led your people,
   to make for yourself a glorious name.

This poetic text is one of a very few in the Old Testament in which the divine presence is called God's "holy spirit." Reflecting upon the events of the exodus, in which God rescued his people from slavery and became their Savior (verse 8), the prophet stated that God's holy spirit was actively present among his people. The one who divided the waters and marched his people through the sea also "put within them his holy spirit" (verse 11). This "spirit of the Lord" led the people through their wilderness wanderings and guided them to their place of rest in God's covenant fulfillment (verse 14). Though the Holy Spirit is not yet described with a separate personal identity, as in the New Testament, already the holy spirit of God is shown to be intimately involved in both the creating and redeeming activity of God, bringing to completion the intentions of God.

Though the people of Israel were guided by God's Spirit in the wilderness, "they rebelled and grieved his holy spirit" (verse 10). In rebelling against God, it is specifically God as holy spirit that they grieved. Paul later took up and expounded this phrase in his New Testament letter, warning his listeners, "Do not grieve the Holy Spirit of God, with which you were marked with a seal for the day of redemption" (Eph 4:30).

The Holy Spirit's role in the history of Israel, then, includes the just and ethical ordering of the people. This is confirmed in a deeply personal way in King David's great lament of Psalm 51. Following his destructive sin, David prays, "Do not take your holy spirit from me" (verse 11). In the context of the lament, taking away the holy spirit means being cast away from God's presence and being deprived of the joy of salvation. Instead, David prays, "Put a new and right spirit within me" (verse 10), and "sustain in me a willing spirit" (verse 12). These aspects of God's spirit within the repentant person describe an individual who is completely new and transformed, with God's life breathing in and through that person.

In these Old Testament texts (Isa 63:10–11; Ps 51:11), two personal dimensions of God's presence—spirit and holiness—are juxtaposed. Holiness is part of the intrinsic nature of God; it is God's primary attribute, God's "otherness." God wanted his own people to be holy also: "Be holy, for I am holy" (Lev 11:44). In the personal, divine title, "holy spirit," God's holiness is joined together with God's gusting power and intimate breath. The Holy Spirit describes God's presence and power, working with his world and his people, to transform and renew. Most often, God's people failed in their attempts to be holy, as God is holy. But there would be One, upon whom God would place his Holy Spirit, who would be the Holy One incarnate. In the One anointed by the Holy Spirit, God would redeem the world.

Reflection and discussion

• How does Isaiah describe the role of the "holy spirit" in the redemption of Israel?

• What does it mean to "grieve" God's Holy Spirit (Isa 63:10; Eph 4:30)?

Not to feel God's presence in you

• How does Psalm 51 describe a renewed and transformed person? How does the Holy Spirit work when I repent of my sin?

joyful to live a life like Jesus; redeemed great faith

• Why is holiness a characteristic first and primarily of God? What does my call to holiness mean to me?

Because it comes from God and he is the perfect role model

Prayer

Come, Holy Spirit, who led God's people through the wilderness and into the land of promise. Blow within me to transform my life, and lead me to the inheritance promised by the Father. Create a new heart within me and restore to me the joy of your salvation.

I will put my spirit within you, and you shall live, and I will place you on your own soil; then you shall know that I, the Lord, have spoken and will act. Ezek 37:14

Promised Renewal through God's Spirit

EZEKIEL 36:24–28; 37:1–14 *24I will take you from the nations, and gather you from all the countries, and bring you into your own land. 25I will sprinkle clean water upon you, and you shall be clean from all your uncleannesses, and from all your idols I will cleanse you. 26A new heart I will give you, and a new spirit I will put within you; and I will remove from your body the heart of stone and give you a heart of flesh. 27I will put my spirit within you, and make you follow my statutes and be careful to observe my ordinances. 28Then you shall live in the land that I gave to your ancestors; and you shall be my people, and I will be your God.*

37 1The hand of the Lord came upon me, and he brought me out by the spirit of the Lord and set me down in the middle of a valley; it was full of bones. 2He led me all round them; there were very many lying in the valley, and they were very dry. 3He said to me, "Mortal, can these bones live?" I answered, "O Lord God, you know." 4Then he said to me, "Prophesy to these bones, and say to them: O dry bones, hear the word of the Lord. 5Thus says the Lord God to these bones: I will cause breath to enter you, and you shall live. 6I will lay sinews on you, and will cause flesh to come upon you, and cover you with skin, and put breath in you, and you shall live; and you shall know that I am the Lord."

[7]So I prophesied as I had been commanded; and as I prophesied, suddenly there was a noise, a rattling, and the bones came together, bone to its bone. [8]I looked, and there were sinews on them, and flesh had come upon them, and skin had covered them; but there was no breath in them. [9]Then he said to me, "Prophesy to the breath, prophesy, mortal, and say to the breath: Thus says the Lord God: Come from the four winds, O breath, and breathe upon these slain, that they may live." [10]I prophesied as he commanded me, and the breath came into them, and they lived, and stood on their feet, a vast multitude.

[11]Then he said to me, "Mortal, these bones are the whole house of Israel. They say, 'Our bones are dried up, and our hope is lost; we are cut off completely.' [12]Therefore prophesy, and say to them, Thus says the Lord God: I am going to open your graves, and bring you up from your graves, O my people; and I will bring you back to the land of Israel. [13]And you shall know that I am the Lord, when I open your graves, and bring you up from your graves, O my people. [14]I will put my spirit within you, and you shall live, and I will place you on your own soil; then you shall know that I, the Lord, have spoken and will act, says the Lord."

Ezekiel's prophecies brought a message of hope to God's people after their nation and temple had been destroyed by the Babylonians. Israel's infidelity and injustice had led to their exile in a foreign land, away from the blessings of God's covenant. Only a miracle of grace could effect a transformation in God's people, so God promised to bring his people back to their own land, to give them a new heart and a new spirit, and to renew the covenant that they had broken. God's promises begin with an external act, "I will sprinkle clean water upon you" (36:25), then follow with an internal gift of renewal, "I will put my spirit within you" (36:27). This symbolic cleansing with water, followed by the interior gift of God's spirit, became the pattern for expressing inner transformation into the Christian era. Israel's experience of covenant renewal—repentance and change of heart, followed by a purifying water ritual, and concluding with the gift of the Spirit—was transformed into the earliest model of Christian initiation into the new covenant. Repentance from sin, baptism in Christ, and the conferral of the Holy Spirit is the expression of God's grace, bringing new life through incorporation into the death and resurrection of Christ.

Ezekiel's vision of the valley of dry bones expressed the hopelessness felt by Israel in the midst of Jerusalem's destruction and their captivity in Babylon—"Our bones are dried up, and our hope is lost; we are cut off completely" (37:11). Yet, God promises that their nation would be brought back to life again and that they would be brought back to live in the land of God's promises. Just as the creation of the world came about through God's word and in the power of his Spirit, here God speaks through the word of his prophet and his energizing Spirit empowers that word, bringing about the new creation of God's people.

The vision is held together by the key Hebrew word, *ruach*—translated either as spirit, breath, or wind, depending on the context, but including all three meanings in every instance. When the word of God spoke, the bones came together and were covered with sinews and flesh. Then God spoke again, invoking the spirit: "Come from the four winds, O breath (*ruach*), and breathe upon these slain, that they may live" (37:9); that is, Come, Spirit, from north and south and east and west and blow. This invocation of God's Spirit is the Old Testament origin of the Christian prayer, "Come, Holy Spirit." God provides the symbolic vision, then he offers us the reality: "I will put my spirit within you and you shall live" (37:14).

Here is a reenactment of the primal act of creation, when God formed humanity from the dust of the ground and blew into his nostrils the breath of life (Gen 2:7). Throughout the Bible, the life-giving breath of God's Spirit moves from individual creation, to the re-creation of the nation, to the promised cosmic renewal of the heavens and the earth. The prayer of Israel becomes the prayer of humanity and of all creation, "Come, Holy Spirit." From the prayer of the early Christians awaiting the day of Pentecost to the epiclesis of every Eucharistic Prayer—"Let your Spirit come upon these gifts to make them holy"—the invocation of the Holy Spirit brings about God's daily new creation among us.

Reflection and discussion

• In what way does God's word weave symbol and reality in this vision of the dry bones? *tired bones were symbolic of the hopelessness felt by Israel in Jerusalem*

• What are the parallels between Israel's experience of covenant renewal and the Christian model for initiation into the new covenant?

repentance   confession
purifying water   baptism
gifts of spirit   confirmula

• When have I felt as if I were in exile: dried up, lost hope, cut off? How did the Spirit bring me renewed life?

• In what way has the prayer of Israel invoking God's Spirit become the prayer of all creation? When and why do I pray, "Come, Holy Spirit"?

Everyone wants the world to be
at pure love

Prayer

Come, Holy Spirit, blow within this incomplete creation the divine breath of new life. Fill up this dried-up and lifeless creation with new life today. Come with your grace and renew the face of the earth.

SUGGESTIONS FOR FACILITATORS, GROUP SESSION 2

1. If there are newcomers who were not present for the first group session, introduce them now.

2. You may want to pray this prayer as a group:
Creating and redeeming God, your word goes forth to all the earth and your Spirit accomplishes your will in all creation. Breathe new life within your people and empower us to manifest your gifts of wisdom, understanding, counsel, fortitude, knowledge, piety, and reverential fear of the Lord. Anoint us with your Spirit, so that we may participate in the mission of your Messiah, to bring justice and peaceful harmony to your world. We wait with trusting hope for the new creation which you have promised, when you will renew the face of the earth.

3. Ask one or both of the following questions:
   • What was your biggest challenge in Bible study over this past week?
   • What did you learn about yourself this week?

4. Discuss lessons 1 through 6 together. Assuming that group members have read the Scripture and commentary during the week, there is no need to read it aloud. As you review each lesson, you might want to briefly summarize the Scripture passages of each lesson and ask the group what stands out most clearly from the commentary.

5. Choose one or more of the questions for reflection and discussion from each lesson to talk over as a group. You may want to ask group members which question was most challenging or helpful to them as you review each lesson.

6. Keep the discussion moving, but don't rush the discussion in order to complete more questions. Allow time for the questions that provoke the most discussion.

7. Instruct group members to complete lessons 7 through 12 on their own during the six days before the next group meeting. They should write out their own answers to the questions as preparation for next week's group discussion.

8. Conclude by praying aloud together the prayer at the end of lesson 6, or any other prayer you choose.

The Holy Spirit will come upon you, and the power of the Most High will overshadow you; therefore the child to be born will be holy; he will be called Son of God. Luke 1:35

Conceived by the Power of the Holy Spirit

LUKE 1:26–45 ²⁶*In the sixth month the angel Gabriel was sent by God to a town in Galilee called Nazareth, ²⁷to a virgin engaged to a man whose name was Joseph, of the house of David. The virgin's name was Mary. ²⁸And he came to her and said, "Greetings, favored one! The Lord is with you." ²⁹But she was much perplexed by his words and pondered what sort of greeting this might be. ³⁰The angel said to her, "Do not be afraid, Mary, for you have found favor with God. ³¹And now, you will conceive in your womb and bear a son, and you will name him Jesus. ³²He will be great, and will be called the Son of the Most High, and the Lord God will give to him the throne of his ancestor David. ³³He will reign over the house of Jacob for ever, and of his kingdom there will be no end." ³⁴Mary said to the angel, "How can this be, since I am a virgin?" ³⁵The angel said to her, "The Holy Spirit will come upon you, and the power of the Most High will over-shadow you; therefore the child to be born will be holy; he will be called Son of God. ³⁶And now, your relative Elizabeth in her old age has also conceived a son; and this is the sixth month for her who was said to be barren. ³⁷For nothing will be impossible with God." ³⁸Then Mary said, "Here am I, the servant of the Lord; let it be with me according to your word." Then the angel departed from her.*

35

[39] In those days Mary set out and went with haste to a Judean town in the hill country, [40] where she entered the house of Zechariah and greeted Elizabeth. [41] When Elizabeth heard Mary's greeting, the child leapt in her womb. And Elizabeth was filled with the Holy Spirit [42] and exclaimed with a loud cry, "Blessed are you among women, and blessed is the fruit of your womb. [43] And why has this happened to me, that the mother of my Lord comes to me? [44] For as soon as I heard the sound of your greeting, the child in my womb leapt for joy. [45] And blessed is she who believed that there would be a fulfillment of what was spoken to her by the Lord."

The inspired writings of Luke (the Gospel According to Luke and the Acts of the Apostles) present the life of Jesus and the life of the church as a dynamic work of the Holy Spirit. The gospel begins with the angelic announcement to Mary that she would be the mother of Jesus by the power of the Holy Spirit. Naturally perplexed by the message, Mary asked, "How can this be, since I am a virgin?" The angel explained, "The Holy Spirit will come upon you, and the power of the Most High will overshadow you" (verses 34–35). Through the bodily motherhood of Mary, God's eternal word would enter time, becoming flesh in the world. From his mother's womb to the empty tomb, Jesus is the man of the Spirit, par excellence.

"The Holy Spirit" and "the power of the Most High" are parallel terms for God's Spirit who would "come upon" Mary and "overshadow" her (verse 35). The Holy Spirit would come upon Mary, just as the Spirit hovered over the waters at the original creation and as the Holy Spirit would later come upon the young church to make it fertile (Acts 1:8). God's Spirit would overshadow Mary, the same language used to describe the cloud overshadowing the tabernacle in the wilderness as it was filled with God's glory (Exod 40:34–35). This is God's new creation and the beginning of God's final work of redemption. Because Mary is a youthful virgin (verse 27), rather than a barren elder like Elizabeth (verse 36), the conception of Jesus by the power of the Holy Spirit is the dawning of a radically new era of God's salvation.

The Holy Spirit manifests God as the One who does what seems impossible (verse 37). Though the angel's announcement to Mary was something far beyond what she could possibly comprehend, Mary accepted it. She welcomed the power of the Holy Spirit into her life: "Let it be with me according to your word" (verse 38). Mary said "yes" to the overshadowing and transforming presence of God's Spirit, and in that acceptance, she became our model for responding to the invitations of the Spirit, for welcoming divine life into us, for bringing the saving presence of Christ into the world. As Mary did at the beginning of the gospel, the whole church would do at the beginning of Acts.

Reflection and discussion

• In what way does Luke's text demonstrate that the conception of Jesus is a thoroughly new creation?

• In what way does the youthful Mary foreshadow the early church? What does the Holy Spirit do in the lives of both Mary and the church?

• What can I learn from Mary about openness to the invitations and promptings of the Holy Spirit?

Prayer

Come, Holy Spirit, overshadow your church just as you entered the life of faithful Mary. Help me open my life to your invitations and promptings and to say "yes" to God's will for me. Make me an instrument of your creative presence in the world.

**Jesus, full of the Holy Spirit, returned from the Jordan
and was led by the Spirit in the wilderness.** Luke 4:1

The Spirit of the Lord
Is upon Me

LUKE 3:21–22 ²¹*Now when all the people were baptized, and when Jesus
also had been baptized and was praying, the heaven was opened,* ²²*and the Holy
Spirit descended upon him in bodily form like a dove. And a voice came from
heaven, "You are my Son, the Beloved; with you I am well pleased."*

LUKE 4:1–2, 13–21 ¹*Jesus, full of the Holy Spirit, returned from the Jordan
and was led by the Spirit in the wilderness,* ²*where for forty days he was tempted
by the devil. He ate nothing at all during those days, and when they were over,
he was famished.*

¹³*When the devil had finished every test, he departed from him until an
opportune time.*

¹⁴*Then Jesus, filled with the power of the Spirit, returned to Galilee, and a
report about him spread through all the surrounding country.* ¹⁵*He began to
teach in their synagogues and was praised by everyone.*

¹⁶*When he came to Nazareth, where he had been brought up, he went to the
synagogue on the sabbath day, as was his custom. He stood up to read,* ¹⁷*and the
scroll of the prophet Isaiah was given to him. He unrolled the scroll and found
the place where it was written:*

18*"The Spirit of the Lord is upon me,*
*   because he has anointed me*
*   to bring good news to the poor.*
He has sent me to proclaim release to the captives
*   and recovery of sight to the blind,*
*   to let the oppressed go free,*
19*to proclaim the year of the Lord's favor."*
20*And he rolled up the scroll, gave it back to the attendant, and sat down. The*
eyes of all in the synagogue were fixed on him. 21*Then he began to say to them,*
"Today this Scripture has been fulfilled in your hearing."

The writings of Luke emphasize that the whole of Jesus' ministry was conducted in the power of the Holy Spirit. At his baptism, "God anointed Jesus of Nazareth with the Holy Spirit and with power" (Acts 10:38). Anointed for his messianic ministry, prefigured by the priests, prophets, and kings of Israel, Jesus possesses the Spirit without measure.

As Jesus came up from the water, the Holy Spirit came down upon him. Luke says that the Spirit descended "in bodily form like a dove" (3:22). The symbol of the dove recalls two images in the early accounts of Genesis. At creation, the Spirit of God "hovered" over the waters (Gen 1:2), which Jewish writings in the Talmud liken to the brooding and fluttering movements of a dove. After the great flood, Noah sent out a dove, which returned with an olive branch after flying over the water, signifying that the destructive water had receded and that new life was arising on the earth. Both images suggest that God is bringing about a new creation through the ministry of Jesus.

The voice from heaven said, "You are my Son, the Beloved; with you I am well pleased." The words allude to Psalm 2:7, a royal enthronement psalm (Acts 13:33), and to Isaiah 42:1, a Servant song—both confirming that Jesus is the anointed Messiah. Together, the word of God and the Spirit of God assure us that Jesus is the one chosen, loved, and empowered by God to do the long-awaited work of creating anew and redeeming humanity.

Immediately after Jesus was anointed with the Holy Spirit, he was led by that same Spirit into the wilderness (4:1). His resistance and faithfulness during the forty days of temptation contrast with Israel's infidelity during their forty years in the wilderness. Though God had "put his holy spirit" within

Israel, "they rebelled and grieved his holy spirit" (Isa 63:10). But Jesus, anointed with the Holy Spirit, overcame the temptations and manifested God's redeeming power throughout his public life.

Returning to Galilee "filled with the power of the Spirit" (4:14), Jesus went to the synagogue of Nazareth and claimed the Servant song of Isaiah as the defining prologue for his whole ministry: "The Spirit of the Lord is upon me, because he has anointed me" (4:18; Isa 61:1). The one empowered by God's Spirit would do the divine work of bringing liberation, healing, and reconciliation. He would fulfill in his present life all that God had promised through the prophets of old (4:21).

The remaining chapters of the gospel demonstrate these authoritative works of Jesus: preaching the good news to the poor, giving freedom to the captives, sight to the blind, hope to the downtrodden. These were the works of the Spirit in his life, the ways he served his Father and did God's saving work. All this is evidence that Jesus is the promised one and that in him the Spirit has come in power. All his works are signs that the final age is upon us, when the Spirit's power will be fully manifested and all the earth will be redeemed and healed.

Reflection and discussion

• The prophets, priests, and kings of the Old Testament were given God's spirit in a measured way for the tasks they were given. How do these events at the inauguration of Jesus' public life demonstrate that Jesus received the fullness of the Holy Spirit in an unmeasured way?

• How does the baptism of Jesus show that God is bringing about a new creation in Jesus Christ?

• How do the temptations of Jesus in the desert demonstrate that God is bringing a new exodus for God's people?

• In what ways are the goals of Jesus' mission continued in the church today (4:18–19)? Which part of Jesus' mission do I continue most effectively?

Prayer

Come, Holy Spirit, anoint me with your power and confidence, as you anointed Jesus. Fortify me to resist temptations and strengthen me to bring good news, healing, and hope to those who need it today.

See, I am sending upon you what my Father promised; so stay here in the city until you have been clothed with power from on high. Luke 24:49

Waiting for What the Father Promised

LUKE 24:44–53 *⁴⁴Then he said to them, "These are my words that I spoke to you while I was still with you—that everything written about me in the law of Moses, the prophets, and the psalms must be fulfilled." ⁴⁵Then he opened their minds to understand the Scriptures, ⁴⁶and he said to them, "Thus it is written, that the Messiah is to suffer and to rise from the dead on the third day, ⁴⁷and that repentance and forgiveness of sins is to be proclaimed in his name to all nations, beginning from Jerusalem. ⁴⁸You are witnesses of these things. ⁴⁹And see, I am sending upon you what my Father promised; so stay here in the city until you have been clothed with power from on high."*

⁵⁰Then he led them out as far as Bethany, and, lifting up his hands, he blessed them. ⁵¹While he was blessing them, he withdrew from them and was carried up into heaven. ⁵²And they worshiped him, and returned to Jerusalem with great joy; ⁵³and they were continually in the temple blessing God.

ACTS 1:1–5 *¹In the first book, Theophilus, I wrote about all that Jesus did and taught from the beginning ²until the day when he was taken up to heaven, after giving instructions through the Holy Spirit to the apostles whom he had chosen. ³After his suffering he presented himself alive to them by many convinc-*

ing proofs, appearing to them over the course of forty days and speaking about the kingdom of God. ⁴While staying with them, he ordered them not to leave Jerusalem, but to wait there for the promise of the Father. "This," he said, "is what you have heard from me; ⁵for John baptized with water, but you will be baptized with the Holy Spirit not many days from now."

The end of Luke's gospel overlaps with the beginning of his Acts of the Apostles. In the gospel, Luke wrote "about all that Jesus did and taught from the beginning until the day when he was taken up to heaven" (Acts 1:1–2). In the Acts, he wrote about all that the church did and taught from its beginning. At the end of the gospel, Jesus told the disciples he would send them what the Father promised and they would be "clothed with power from on high" (Luke 24:49). At the beginning of Acts, Jesus reminds the disciples to wait for "the promise of the Father," which will be given as they are "baptized with the Holy Spirit" (Acts 1:4–5).

Luke demonstrated in his gospel that all the activities of Jesus were directed by the Holy Spirit, through whom he had been conceived and by whom he was anointed. Luke shows in the Acts that the church is empowered and directed by this same Holy Spirit, through whom the church is conceived and by whom his disciples are baptized. Truly, this two-volume work is united through the dynamic action of God's Spirit.

Immediately before the departure of Jesus from his disciples, he "opened their minds to understand the Scriptures," helping them understand those things written about Jesus in the Torah of Moses, the prophets, and the psalms (Luke 24:45). These Jewish Scriptures, when interpreted in light of the Messiah, contain a message and a challenge that constitute the foundation of the Christian church. The message is "that the Messiah is to suffer and to rise from the dead on the third day"; the challenge is "that repentance and forgiveness of sins is to be proclaimed in his name to all nations" (Luke 24:46–47). In fact, this message and challenge form the two major issues with which we see the church struggling in the Acts of the Apostles: preaching a Messiah who both suffers and dies and welcoming non-Jews into the reconciled community without distinction. And, if we are honest, this message and challenge are still the two most difficult issues that the church faces two millennia later: proclaiming a crucified Christ and accepting people of all nations equally. Yet, the Holy Spirit continues to empower the church for this mission and enlighten disciples to understand the Scriptures.

The two great figures of the Torah and the prophets, Moses and Elijah, each transmitted their "spirit" to their successors at their departure. Because Moses laid his hands on Joshua, his successor, Joshua was filled with the spirit of wisdom and did as God had commanded Moses (Deut 34:9). Before Elijah ascended to heaven, Elisha, his successor, asked for a double share of his spirit. So when Elijah departed, his spirit was actively present in his successor (2 Kings 2:9, 15). Likewise, as Jesus departs, he promises his Spirit to his disciples. The Acts of the Apostles will demonstrate that the work of Jesus continues in the church through the power of the Holy Spirit.

Reflection and discussion

• Why is the Acts of the Apostles sometimes referred to as the gospel of the Holy Spirit? In what way is the Holy Spirit the power that unites the gospel and Acts?

• In what way have I experienced the Holy Spirit opening my mind to understand the Scriptures?

Prayer

Come, Holy Spirit, direct your church to proclaim the message of Christ crucified and risen. Empower your disciples to proclaim repentance and forgiveness to all people. Show me how to do the work of Jesus in the world today.

You will receive power when the Holy Spirit has come upon you;
and you will be my witnesses in Jerusalem, in all Judea and Samaria,
and to the ends of the earth. Acts 1:8

The Holy Spirit Will Make You Witnesses

ACTS 1:6–14 ⁶*So when they had come together, they asked him, "Lord, is this the time when you will restore the kingdom to Israel?"* ⁷*He replied, "It is not for you to know the times or periods that the Father has set by his own authority.* ⁸*But you will receive power when the Holy Spirit has come upon you; and you will be my witnesses in Jerusalem, in all Judea and Samaria, and to the ends of the earth."* ⁹*When he had said this, as they were watching, he was lifted up, and a cloud took him out of their sight.* ¹⁰*While he was going and they were gazing up towards heaven, suddenly two men in white robes stood by them.* ¹¹*They said, "Men of Galilee, why do you stand looking up toward heaven? This Jesus, who has been taken up from you into heaven, will come in the same way as you saw him go into heaven."* ¹²*Then they returned to Jerusalem from the mount called Olivet, which is near Jerusalem, a sabbath day's journey away.* ¹³*When they had entered the city, they went to the room upstairs where they were staying, Peter, and John, and James, and Andrew, Philip and Thomas, Bartholomew and Matthew, James son of Alphaeus, and Simon the Zealot, and Judas son of James.* ¹⁴*All these were constantly devoting themselves to prayer, together with certain women, including Mary the mother of Jesus, as well as his brothers.*

When the disciples met with the risen Jesus, they were filled with hope and yearning. They wanted Christ to finish the work he had begun, to fulfill his promise to restore God's kingdom (verse 6). The reply of Jesus was twofold: first, he told them that they cannot know "the times or periods that the Father has set," ending their speculation about the end of the age (verse 7); and second, he told them that they would be his "witnesses" in the world (verse 8). The promised kingdom would be fully restored as a gift in God's own time, but in the meantime, they were not to wait idly, but to be witnesses filled with joyful hope in the promises Jesus had left them.

The ascension of Jesus meant that the disciples' understanding of the world was now different. They recognized that the one who had taught, healed, and loved them had been raised to rule with the world's Creator. In this new reality, the future is still to be fully realized; it is open-ended to the movements of God's Spirit. The disciples are not to stand gazing up toward heaven, for the presence of Jesus will be with them in the spiritual outpouring they will soon receive. They should return to the city to await their empowerment by the Holy Spirit for their witness, for the same force which empowered Jesus would be present in his church.

The time between the ascension and Pentecost is a significant pause between God's mighty acts, a pause in which the church's task is to wait and to pray, "Come, Holy Spirit." The witness of disciples must be more than just earnest striving and busy activity. They must await God's grace with expectant hearts. Jesus had taught them "to pray always and not to lose heart" (Luke 18:1). "Ask, and it will be given to you....How much more will the heavenly Father give the Holy Spirit to those who ask him" (Luke 11:9, 13).

The scene of the church at prayer is an image of what Christ's church is called to be. The male and female disciples of Jesus were praying together, joined by Mary, the mother of Jesus (verse 14). Waiting and praying teach us that God's gift of the Spirit is never our assured possession. God's Spirit must be constantly sought anew in prayer. For Luke, the figure of Mary is a model for the kind of expectant faith in God's promises which Jesus wants for the church: "Blessed is she who believed that there would be a fulfillment of what was spoken to her by the Lord" (Luke 1:45). Luke began his gospel by showing us the figure of Mary overshadowed by the Holy Spirit to give birth to Jesus; so he begins Acts with Mary awaiting the coming of the Spirit to give birth to the church.

Reflection and discussion

• What is the task of disciples between the time of Jesus' ascension and his return in glory? What do I need to learn about living in the interim?

• Why is waiting and praying just as important for the church as projects and activities? Which do I do best?

• What do Mary and the other disciples have to teach me about being a witness to Jesus?

Prayer

Come, Holy Spirit, teach me how to wait and pray for the experience of your outpouring. Transform me with your grace into the image of Jesus, so that I may bear witness to him. Help me to await Christ's return with joyful hope.

In the last days it will be, God declares,
that I will pour out my Spirit upon all flesh,
and your sons and your daughters shall prophesy,
and your young men shall see visions,
and your old men shall dream dreams. Acts 2:17

Pouring out the Holy Spirit of God

ACTS 2:1–21 ¹*When the day of Pentecost had come, they were all together in one place. ²And suddenly from heaven there came a sound like the rush of a violent wind, and it filled the entire house where they were sitting. ³Divided tongues, as of fire, appeared among them, and a tongue rested on each of them. ⁴All of them were filled with the Holy Spirit and began to speak in other languages, as the Spirit gave them ability.*

⁵Now there were devout Jews from every nation under heaven living in Jerusalem. ⁶And at this sound the crowd gathered and was bewildered, because each one heard them speaking in the native language of each. ⁷Amazed and astonished, they asked, "Are not all these who are speaking Galileans? ⁸And how is it that we hear, each of us, in our own native language? ⁹Parthians, Medes, Elamites, and residents of Mesopotamia, Judea and Cappadocia, Pontus and Asia, ¹⁰Phrygia and Pamphylia, Egypt and the parts of Libya belonging to Cyrene, and visitors from Rome, both Jews and proselytes, ¹¹Cretans and Arabs—in our own languages we hear them speaking about God's deeds of power." [12]*All were amazed and perplexed, saying to one another, "What does this mean?"* [13]*But others sneered and said, "They are filled with new wine."*

[14]*But Peter, standing with the eleven, raised his voice and addressed them: "Men of Judea and all who live in Jerusalem, let this be known to you, and listen to what I say.* [15]*Indeed, these are not drunk, as you suppose, for it is only nine o'clock in the morning.* [16]*No, this is what was spoken through the prophet Joel:*

[17]*'In the last days it will be, God declares,*
that I will pour out my Spirit upon all flesh,
and your sons and your daughters shall prophesy,
and your young men shall see visions,
and your old men shall dream dreams.
[18]*Even upon my slaves, both men and women,*
in those days I will pour out my Spirit;
and they shall prophesy.
[19]*And I will show portents in the heaven above*
and signs on the earth below,
blood, and fire, and smoky mist.
[20]*The sun shall be turned to darkness*
and the moon to blood,
before the coming of the Lord's great and glorious day.
[21]*Then everyone who calls on the name of the Lord shall be saved.'"*

The event of Pentecost is intimately united with the saving life of Christ. Luke shows that Pentecost is the last of three stages in Jesus' relationship with the Spirit. The first begins with his conception by Mary through the power of the Holy Spirit (Luke 1:35). The second begins with Christ's baptism, when he is anointed with the Spirit and confirmed as the Messiah (Luke 3:22). The third begins with his death and resurrection, and it is unfolded in his ascension and Pentecost. The one who was first filled with the Holy Spirit now sends the Spirit and clothes his disciples "with power from on high" (Luke 24:49).

John the Baptist had announced that Jesus would baptize "with the Holy Spirit and fire" (Luke 3:16). But Jesus himself would first undergo a baptism of fire in his passion and death for us. His own words testify to that fire for which his whole emotional life prepared: "I came to bring fire to the earth, and how I wish it were already kindled! I have a baptism with which to be baptized, and what stress I am under until it is completed!" (Luke 12:49–50). Because Jesus himself was baptized with fire in the destructive power of the cross, the fire of Pentecost became the power of God's gracious gift.

The day of Pentecost began with an eruption of sound like a rushing wind. The same wind that swept over the waters on the first day of creation (Gen 1:2) was producing a new creation. God was putting "a new spirit," God's own Spirit, within his people (Ezek 36:26–27). Not only was God creating his people anew, but the Spirit was resting upon each person as they began to speak fearlessly. The very first to speak was Peter. The same spirit which God blew into the dust to create a human being (Gen 2:7) now breathed life into this once cowardly disciple and created a new man. The same Peter who only a few weeks before could not speak up when his master was on trial now proclaims the message of Christ in the power of the Holy Spirit (verse 14).

The effects of sin, represented by the confusion of Babel (Gen 11:1–9), began to be reversed at Pentecost. At Babel, the one language of humanity became confused so that people could not understand one another and scattered over the face of the earth. At Pentecost, the one gospel began to be heard and understood in the languages of "every nation under heaven" (verse 5). The fiery "tongues" became the gift of "other tongues" as they began to speak under the promptings of the Holy Spirit (verse 4). In the words of St. Irenaeus, "All tongues together, of one accord, then raised up a hymn to God." Once again, God's Spirit was bringing order out of confusion, creation out of chaos, so that the disciples could be witnesses of Christ all over the world.

Peter's proclamation from the prophet Joel indicates that God's promises were being fulfilled as the Holy Spirit is poured out without measure (verses 17–18). In previous ages, the Spirit had been given in measured form to prophets, priests, and kings. Now, through the saving death and resurrection of God's Messiah, all God's people experienced the manifestations of God's Spirit—sons and daughters, men and women, young and old, slaves and free people. What Moses had longed for was now a reality: "Would that all the Lord's people were prophets, and that the Lord would put his spirit on them!" (Num 11:29). Now all God's people share in the prophetic, priestly, and kingly anointing of Christ through sharing in his Spirit.

Reflection and discussion

• What symbolic manifestations of the Spirit indicate that Pentecost is a new creation?

• What is the relationship of the feasts of the Annunciation, the baptism of Jesus, and Pentecost? Why is Pentecost the conclusion of the liturgical season of Easter?

• In what way was Peter affected by the power of the Holy Spirit? In what similar ways has God's Spirit transformed my life?

Prayer

Come, Holy Spirit, take away my timid and cowardly spirit and give me a spirit of courage and fervor. Sanctify my heart for the glory of God's kingdom and kindle in me the fire of your divine love.

When Paul had laid his hands on them, the Holy Spirit came upon them, and they spoke in tongues and prophesied. Acts 19:6

All Are Filled with the Spirit

ACTS 10:44–48 ⁴*While Peter was still speaking, the Holy Spirit fell upon all who heard the word.* ⁴⁵*The circumcised believers who had come with Peter were astounded that the gift of the Holy Spirit had been poured out even on the Gentiles,* ⁴⁶*for they heard them speaking in tongues and extolling God. Then Peter said,* ⁴⁷*"Can anyone withhold the water for baptizing these people who have received the Holy Spirit just as we have?"* ⁴⁸*So he ordered them to be baptized in the name of Jesus Christ. Then they invited him to stay for several days.*

ACTS 19:1–7 ¹*While Apollos was in Corinth, Paul passed through the inland regions and came to Ephesus, where he found some disciples.* ²*He said to them, "Did you receive the Holy Spirit when you became believers?" They replied, "No, we have not even heard that there is a Holy Spirit."* ³*Then he said, "Into what then were you baptized?" They answered, "Into John's baptism."* ⁴*Paul said, "John baptized with the baptism of repentance, telling the people to believe in the one who was to come after him, that is, in Jesus."* ⁵*On hearing this, they were baptized in the name of the Lord Jesus.* ⁶*When Paul had laid his hands on them, the Holy Spirit came upon them, and they spoke in tongues and prophesied—* ⁷*altogether there were about twelve of them.*

Since the faith of Jesus and his disciples was rooted in Israel, the earliest church was totally Jewish. The Christians continued to go to the temple in Jerusalem to pray, and they continued to follow the Torah of Moses with its ritual and dietary laws. One of the most difficult questions that faced the early church was whether non-Jews (Gentiles) could become Christians. Since Jesus had given no explicit instructions about this matter, it was left to the guidance of the Holy Spirit to resolve the issue.

The Spirit guided Peter to the house of Cornelius, a Gentile army officer, having prepared him through a vision (Acts 10). When Peter began to speak to the household of Cornelius, he explained that the Spirit had led him to understand the full implications of the gospel: "that God shows no partiality" because Jesus Christ is "Lord of all" (10:34–36). After Peter spoke about the saving truth of Christ, he and his Jewish companions were astonished to see that the gift of the Holy Spirit was poured out on Cornelius and his household just as the Spirit had come on the disciples at Pentecost in Jerusalem (10:45). Surely the Spirit was telling the church that it must be open to all who believe in Jesus, Gentile as well as Jew.

Throughout Acts, the Holy Spirit is shown compelling the church outward, breaking down previously-held boundaries. If Jesus Christ is truly the Lord of all, then the church has the ongoing task of penetrating new dimensions of its Spirit-led calling to be witnesses to the ends of the earth (1:8). The church of our day, like the church of Acts, must expect to be led in new and surprising ways as it takes its lead from the guidance and prodding of the Holy Spirit.

When Paul traveled to Ephesus, he met twelve disciples who had not yet been baptized into Christ. They had only received the preparatory baptism of John the Baptist, the baptism of repentance that preceded the coming of Christ's Spirit (19:3–4). Paul then baptized them "in the name of the Lord Jesus" and laid his hands upon them so that they would receive the Holy Spirit (19:5–6). Through Christian baptism, these twelve disciples passed personally from the era of expectation to the new covenant of redemption.

What took place in the house of Cornelius and in Ephesus was not a new Pentecost, for Pentecost cannot be repeated any more than the death and resurrection of Christ can be repeated. But the grace of Pentecost is made present again in the life of every believer who enters into the experience of baptism. Through baptism into Christ and the laying on of hands, the Holy

Spirit of Pentecost fills the life of the Christian. The Spirit, given by Christ in his death and resurrection and manifested to the church at Pentecost, is poured out into our hearts and manifests God's spiritual gifts within us. The earthquake which had its epicenter at Pentecost continues to create after-shocks and rumblings down through the ages as the Spirit continues to come in power to all who put their faith in Jesus and allow the grace of baptism to be active in their lives.

Reflection and discussion

• The Holy Spirit guided the church to receive the Gentiles into the Christian faith. In what other issues does the Spirit continue to guide the church?

• The Holy Spirit guided Peter to understand that Jesus is "Lord of all" because God shows no partiality. In what way does this understanding challenge me to break down previously erected boundaries?

Prayer

Come, Holy Spirit, come with your grace and fill the hearts you have made. May the divine power released into the world at Pentecost be stirred up in my heart. Send your gifts upon your people so that your church may witness to Jesus Christ to the ends of the earth.

SUGGESTIONS FOR FACILITATORS, GROUP SESSION 3

1. Welcome group members and ask if there are any announcements anyone would like to make.

2. You may want to pray this prayer as a group:
Saving God, you filled Jesus Christ will the power of the Holy Spirit and you poured out that same Spirit upon the church at Pentecost. Kindle in your church the fire of the Holy Spirit so that we may witness your saving love to the whole world. Help us break down the boundaries that divide people from one another and realize your desire to fill all people with your Spirit. As we study your sacred Scriptures, encourage us and guide us with the inspiration of your Holy Spirit.

3. Ask one or both of the following questions:
   • Which image from the lessons this week stands out most memorably to you?
   • What is the most important lesson you learned through your study this week?

4. Discuss lessons 7 through 12. Choose one or more of the questions for reflection and discussion from each lesson to discuss as a group. You may want to ask group members which question was most challenging or helpful to them as you review each lesson.

5. Remember that there are no definitive answers for these discussion questions. The insights of group members will add to the understanding of all. None of these questions require an expert.

6. After talking about each lesson, instruct group members to complete lessons 13 through 18 on their own during the six days before the next group meeting. They should write out their own answers to the questions as preparation for next week's group discussion.

7. Ask the group if anyone is having any particular problems with the Bible study during the week. You may want to share advice and encouragement within the group.

8. Conclude by praying aloud together the prayer at the end of one of the lessons discussed. You may add to the prayer based on the sharing that has occurred in the group.

He on whom you see the Spirit descend and remain is the one who baptizes with the Holy Spirit. John 1:33

Descending from Heaven Like a Dove

JOHN 1:19–34 ¹⁹*This is the testimony given by John when the Jews sent priests and Levites from Jerusalem to ask him, "Who are you?" ²⁰He confessed and did not deny it, but confessed, "I am not the Messiah." ²¹And they asked him, "What then? Are you Elijah?" He said, "I am not." "Are you the prophet?" He answered, "No." ²²Then they said to him, "Who are you? Let us have an answer for those who sent us. What do you say about yourself?" ²³He said,*

"I am the voice of one crying out in the wilderness,
'Make straight the way of the Lord,'"
as the prophet Isaiah said.

²⁴*Now they had been sent from the Pharisees. ²⁵They asked him, "Why then are you baptizing if you are neither the Messiah, nor Elijah, nor the prophet?" ²⁶John answered them, "I baptize with water. Among you stands one whom you do not know, ²⁷the one who is coming after me; I am not worthy to untie the thong of his sandal." ²⁸This took place in Bethany across the Jordan where John was baptizing.*

²⁹*The next day he saw Jesus coming toward him and declared, "Here is the Lamb of God who takes away the sin of the world! ³⁰This is he of whom I said, 'After me comes a man who ranks ahead of me because he was before me.' ³¹I*

myself did not know him; but I came baptizing with water for this reason, that he might be revealed to Israel." ³²And John testified, "I saw the Spirit descending from heaven like a dove, and it remained on him. ³³I myself did not know him, but the one who sent me to baptize with water said to me, 'He on whom you see the Spirit descend and remain is the one who baptizes with the Holy Spirit.' ³⁴And I myself have seen and have testified that this is the Son of God."

The Gospel of John presents the coming of Christ into the world as a new creation, a new beginning for the world. The gospel opens with the same words which introduce the creation account of Genesis, "in the beginning" (Gen 1:1; John 1:1). The word of God, which first spoke the world into being, has now become flesh to live among us (1:14). The light that illumined every creature from the beginning has now come into the world in Jesus Christ (1:5). That Light of the world continues to confront the darkness and shine into the shadows of sin, hopelessness, and death.

The Spirit of God, which hovered over the waters at creation, has descended from heaven like a dove and remained on Christ (verse 32). Jesus is that Servant of God about whom God had promised, "I have put my spirit upon him" (Isa 42:1). He is the Messiah, about whom God had revealed, "The spirit of the Lord shall rest on him" (Isa 11:2). From his baptism, Jesus was full of the Spirit, enabling him to carry out his mission as God's chosen one.

The role of John the Baptist was to prepare the people for Christ and to announce his entrance upon the scene. When John was baptizing with water, God revealed the identity of his Son to him: "He on whom you see the Spirit descend and remain is the one who baptizes with the Holy Spirit" (verse 33). Because John had "seen" the Spirit descend and remain on Jesus, John could announce his arrival, "Here is the Lamb of God who takes away the sin of the world!" (verse 29), and testify that "this is the Son of God" (verse 34).

In all four gospels, John points to Jesus and tells his listeners, "He is the one who is going to baptize with the Holy Spirit" (Matt 3:11; Mark 1:8; Luke 3:16; John 1:33). Bringing the Holy Spirit to us is at the heart of the mission of Jesus. But before he can bestow the Spirit upon us, he must first be possessed by the Spirit fully and then be led by the Spirit throughout his messianic work. Not only does the Holy Spirit descend on Jesus, the Spirit "remains" on him. This same verb is used in the gospel to describe the permanent, abiding relationship between the Son and the Father and between Jesus and believers. This presentation of the Holy Spirit which descends and remains unfolds as John's gospel continues.

Reflection and discussion

• What is the role of John the Baptist in John's gospel? In what way does the Holy Spirit help me recognize Christ and witness to him?

To announce the
John was to prepare people for
Christ and announce his arrival

• John recognized the Coming One as the one on whom the Spirit descended and remained. How do I recognize the presence of God's Spirit?

beauty of nature
Kindness of people
humility

• Which of the names of Jesus in John 1 help increase my faith in him: the Word, the Light, the Messiah, the Prophet, the Lamb of God, the Son of God? How does the Holy Spirit help me know Jesus better?

Lamb of God son of God

Prayer

Come, Holy Spirit, give me the courage and insight to be a witness for Christ. As you descended and remained on Jesus the Messiah, come into my heart so that I may truly know Jesus and follow him as a devoted disciple.

The wind blows where it chooses, and you hear the sound of it,
but you do not know where it comes from or where it goes.
So it is with everyone who is born of the Spirit. John 3:8

Born of the Spirit

JOHN 3:1–12 ¹*Now there was a Pharisee named Nicodemus, a leader of the Jews. ²He came to Jesus by night and said to him, "Rabbi, we know that you are a teacher who has come from God; for no one can do these signs that you do apart from the presence of God." ³Jesus answered him, "Very truly, I tell you, no one can see the kingdom of God without being born from above." ⁴Nicodemus said to him, "How can anyone be born after having grown old? Can one enter a second time into the mother's womb and be born?" ⁵Jesus answered, "Very truly, I tell you, no one can enter the kingdom of God without being born of water and Spirit. ⁶What is born of the flesh is flesh, and what is born of the Spirit is spirit. ⁷Do not be astonished that I said to you, 'You must be born from above.' ⁸The wind blows where it chooses, and you hear the sound of it, but you do not know where it comes from or where it goes. So it is with everyone who is born of the Spirit." ⁹Nicodemus said to him, "How can these things be?" ¹⁰Jesus answered him, "Are you a teacher of Israel, and yet you do not understand these things?*

¹¹*"Very truly, I tell you, we speak of what we know and testify to what we have seen; yet you do not receive our testimony. ¹²If I have told you about earthly things and you do not believe, how can you believe if I tell you about heavenly things?"*

JOHN 7:37–39 *37On the last day of the festival, the great day, while Jesus was standing there, he cried out, "Let anyone who is thirsty come to me, 38and let the one who believes in me drink. As the Scripture has said, 'Out of the believer's heart shall flow rivers of living water.'" 39Now he said this about the Spirit, which believers in him were to receive; for as yet there was no Spirit, because Jesus was not yet glorified.*

Through the character of Nicodemus, who comes from the darkness toward the Light of the world (verse 1), Jesus presents the essence of the new life he offers. Nicodemus has been attracted to Jesus through his teachings and the signs he has performed, but Jesus tells him that experiencing the kingdom of God requires nothing less than a new birth (verses 2–3). The Greek adverb that describes this new birth has a double meaning: it means born "again" and born "from above." Nicodemus assumes that Jesus is talking about being born again, in a temporal sense, and he cannot understand how this could be possible (verse 4). But Jesus explains further that a person must be "born of water and Spirit" (verse 5). Entry into the Christian life involved a temporal, human experience of water, and a spiritual, divine experience of the Holy Spirit. Christian baptism, as presented throughout the New Testament, involves both of these elements.

The metaphor of new birth expresses the radical, personal transformation involved in initiation into the community of faith formed around Jesus. In another place, Jesus had used the image of becoming like a little child as metaphor of discipleship: "Unless you change and become like children, you will never enter the kingdom" (Matt 18:3). But John's gospel declares that entering God's kingdom requires the more far-reaching experience of rebirth. We are powerless to enter this new life in the weakness and frailty of human flesh; it requires the action of God's Spirit (verse 6). We are no more able to bring ourselves into the kingdom than we are able to be conceived and born unaided. We are radically dependent on the gift and the power of the Holy Spirit.

Jesus expresses the new life of Christian discipleship as "seeing" (verse 3) and "entering" (verse 5) the kingdom of God. Discipleship is the realm of the Spirit, in which believers become children of God as a result of God's initiative and the gift of grace. This regeneration which comes through initiation into the life of salvation involves the whole person. There is no part of life that remains uninfluenced by the Spirit's renewing work. Our minds are enlightened, our wills are liberated, our hearts are made new, and even our bodies will eventually be transformed through the resurrection. Seeing and entering the kingdom is an experience that begins with baptism, continues throughout the Christian life, and is perfected in eternity.

Jesus responds to the astonishment of Nicodemus by explaining that the Spirit is a mystery beyond human control or understanding (verses 7-8). Since the same Greek word means both "wind" and "Spirit," Jesus compares the nature of the Holy Spirit with the actions of the wind. We cannot know the origin and destiny of God's Spirit or understand its unfathomable quality; it is beyond our control or comprehension. We can only experience the Spirit's effects. Thus, "everyone who is born of the Spirit" enters into a life that is totally new, a life that God has breathed into our lives from his own and which moves us in fresh and unexpected ways.

Jesus later describes the life of the newborn Christian using the image of flowing water: "Out of the believer's heart shall flow rivers of living water" (7:38). This image describes, first of all, the heart of Jesus. But when the Holy Spirit is given after Jesus is glorified, it describes also the heart of the Christian who is born from above. The "rivers of living water" flowing from the believer's heart expresses the Holy Spirit and the refreshing experience of living in the Spirit.

Reflection and discussion

• In what ways have I experienced my Christian life as a new birth? What challenges does the image of new birth in the Spirit present for me?

• In what ways do I experience the Spirit's renewing work throughout my whole self: mind, will, heart, and body?

• Why does Jesus use the image of wind and flowing water to describe life in the Holy Spirit?

• In what way do I experience life in the Spirit as unpredictable and unfathomable? In which direction is God's Spirit blowing today?

Prayer

Come, Holy Spirit, give me new life as you stir up the grace of baptism within me. Blow within my life in whichever direction you choose and keep me open to respond to your mysterious presence and movements. Open my heart to you so that the waters of life may flow through me, cleansing, refreshing, and giving me abundant and eternal life.

This is the Spirit of truth, whom the world cannot receive, because it neither sees him nor knows him. You know him, because he abides with you, and he will be in you. John 14:17

The Advocate Will Teach You Everything

JOHN 14:15–26 [15]*"If you love me, you will keep my commandments.* [16]*And I will ask the Father, and he will give you another Advocate, to be with you for ever.* [17]*This is the Spirit of truth, whom the world cannot receive, because it neither sees him nor knows him. You know him, because he abides with you, and he will be in you.*

[18]*"I will not leave you orphaned; I am coming to you.* [19]*In a little while the world will no longer see me, but you will see me; because I live, you also will live.* [20]*On that day you will know that I am in my Father, and you in me, and I in you.* [21]*They who have my commandments and keep them are those who love me; and those who love me will be loved by my Father, and I will love them and reveal myself to them."* [22]*Judas (not Iscariot) said to him, "Lord, how is it that you will reveal yourself to us, and not to the world?"* [23]*Jesus answered him, "Those who love me will keep my word, and my Father will love them, and we will come to them and make our home with them.* [24]*Whoever does not love me does not keep my words; and the word that you hear is not mine, but is from the Father who sent me.*

^{25}"*I have said these things to you while I am still with you.* ^{26}*But the Advocate, the Holy Spirit, whom the Father will send in my name, will teach you every- thing, and remind you of all that I have said to you.*"

As the earthly life of Jesus draws to a close and he prepares his disciples for his departure and return to the Father, Jesus promises his disciples that he will not leave them orphans (verse 18). Because they have been born from above and have become children of the Father, they will expe- rience the loving intimacy of God's family even more closely: "You will know that I am in my Father, and you in me, and I in you" (verse 20). Even though Jesus is departing from them, he promises that he will come to them and remain with them through his Holy Spirit. This abiding presence of Jesus, even in his absence, is the work of the Spirit, whom Jesus promises will be "with" and "in" his disciples (verse 17). In this new era of the Spirit, the living Jesus will be closer to his disciples than ever before.

In this section of John's gospel, Jesus calls the Holy Spirit the "Paraclete," a Greek word which literally means "one called to the side of another." Paraclete is translated in various ways: Advocate, Helper, Counselor, Comforter, and Consoler (verses 16, 26). The Spirit will do for the disciples what Jesus himself did for them when he was living in their midst—especially teaching and encouraging them. The Paraclete will illuminate the revelation from God that Jesus brought and apply it to the ever-changing needs of the community.

The Paraclete is also called "the Spirit of truth" (verse 17). Jesus came to reveal to us the ultimate truth, the truth of the Father's love experienced by Jesus and manifested in his life, death, and resurrection. We are invited to par- ticipate in this truth by becoming one with Jesus through faith. The Spirit of truth is instinctively and interiorly experienced as an abiding presence by those who follow the glorified Jesus. Through believing in Jesus, loving him, and keeping his commandments, the disciples receive the Holy Spirit. The physical departure of Jesus does not end his real presence or the ongoing rev- elation of God in Jesus.

This presence of the Holy Spirit, "whom the world cannot receive" (verse 17), is unable to be "seen" in the usual and worldly sense of the term (verse 19). For that reason, Judas asks Jesus why the disciples and the world see things so differently (verse 22). Jesus explains that those who do not accept God's loving invitation cannot experience the Spirit of truth, the ongoing presence and revelation of God. The Spirit is first of all a gift from God, but a gift that must be accepted through one's loving, active response to God's word. Contrary to outward appearances, Jesus and the Father will make their home with the disciples (verse 23) in and through the Holy Spirit who will be with them forever.

Reflection and discussion

• What is the meaning of Paraclete? In what way have I experienced the Holy Spirit as the Paraclete?

• In response to the question of Judas (verse 22), how does Jesus describe the difference between the church and the world of unbelievers? How do I see what the world cannot see (verse 19)?

• In what way have I experienced the Holy Spirit teaching me and reminding me (verse 26) as I study the Scriptures?

Prayer

Come, Holy Spirit, be my Advocate, Helper, Counselor, and Consoler. Continue to teach me and remind me of everything that Jesus has revealed. Guide me as I read the Scriptures and remain with me always.

When the Spirit of truth comes, he will guide you into all the truth;
for he will not speak on his own, but will speak whatever he hears,
and he will declare to you the things that are to come. John 16:13

The Spirit Will Guide You to All the Truth

JOHN 16:4–15 ⁴*"But I have said these things to you so that when their hour comes you may remember that I told you about them.*

"I did not say these things to you from the beginning, because I was with you. ⁵*But now I am going to him who sent me; yet none of you asks me, 'Where are you going?'* ⁶*But because I have said these things to you, sorrow has filled your hearts.* ⁷*Nevertheless, I tell you the truth: it is to your advantage that I go away, for if I do not go away, the Advocate will not come to you; but if I go, I will send him to you.* ⁸*And when he comes, he will prove the world wrong about sin and righteousness and judgement:* ⁹*about sin, because they do not believe in me;* ¹⁰*about righteousness, because I am going to the Father and you will see me no longer;* ¹¹*about judgement, because the ruler of this world has been condemned.*

¹²*"I still have many things to say to you, but you cannot bear them now.* ¹³*When the Spirit of truth comes, he will guide you into all the truth; for he will not speak on his own, but will speak whatever he hears, and he will declare to you the things that are to come.* ¹⁴*He will glorify me, because he will take what is mine and declare it to you.* ¹⁵*All that the Father has is mine. For this reason I said that he will take what is mine and declare it to you."*

Our lives are filled with goodbyes—the farewell of children leaving home, the departure of friends moving away, and the inevitable separation of death. The human experience of continual parting would fill our lives with constant sorrow were it not for the hope-filled existence we have been given in Christ. Upon his departure from them, Jesus says to his disciples, "Sorrow has filled your hearts" (verse 6). Yet, amazingly, Jesus also says to them, "It is to your advantage that I go away" (verse 7). The earthly attachment of Jesus and his disciples had to end, but only to create a bond that would never end, an attachment of the disciples to Jesus and the Father through the Holy Spirit.

The Paraclete (Advocate) is the glorified Jesus made present when he is absent. The Spirit is the eternal presence of the divine Christ with believers, the fulfillment of his promises to dwell with his disciples. Though it might seem attractive to have been with Jesus during his earthly life, there is no doubt that Jesus is more present to us now in the Spirit than he ever was to his disciples during his earthly life. In those days, Jesus lived *with* his disciples; after he is glorified, Jesus lives *in* his disciples through the Spirit.

The Spirit of truth will guide believers "into all the truth" (verse 13). If our understanding of Jesus were limited to only what Jesus was able to convey to his followers during his public life on earth, our belief would be as inadequate as that of the disciples before the resurrection. But the Holy Spirit enlightens disciples to understand and experience the truth of Christ much more richly. Because of the Spirit, Jesus is not a distant figure from the past; he is the living Lord of our lives. Through the Spirit of truth, the whole mystery of Jesus—his words, actions, death, and resurrection—will be more completely comprehended, interiorized, and lived.

The gift of the Spirit signals a new stage in the history of salvation. After the resurrection of Jesus and before his final coming in glory, the community of disciples experience Christ in the sacramental worship and Spirit-guided teaching of the church. During this age of the church, the Holy Spirit reminds disciples of all that Jesus has said (14:26) and declares "the things that are to come" (verse 13). The disciples' journey "into all the truth" is not yet complete. The "many things" (verse 12) that Jesus did not tell his disciples during his earthly life will gradually be revealed through the work of the Spirit in the ongoing life of Christ's church.

Reflection and discussion

• What is the meaning of Jesus' astonishing words to his disciples, "It is to your advantage that I go away" (verse 7)?

• In what way can it be said that Jesus is more present with me now than he was with his disciples on earth? What are the results of this intimacy with Jesus in my own life?

• Why was Jesus unable to say to his disciples many of the things he had to tell them (verse 12)? In what way does the Holy Spirit, present in the community of disciples, guide the church "into all the truth" (verse 13)?

Prayer

Come, Holy Spirit, empower your church to transform our world with your truth. Guide me into the fullness of truth and help me comprehend the mystery of Christ in all its richness and depth.

As you, Father, are in me and I am in you, may they also be in us, so that the world may believe that you have sent me. John 17:21

That They May All Be One

JOHN 17:11–26 [11]*And now I am no longer in the world, but they are in the world, and I am coming to you. Holy Father, protect them in your name that you have given me, so that they may be one, as we are one.* [12]*While I was with them, I protected them in your name that you have given me. I guarded them, and not one of them was lost except the one destined to be lost, so that the Scripture might be fulfilled.* [13]*But now I am coming to you, and I speak these things in the world so that they may have my joy made complete in themselves.* [14]*I have given them your word, and the world has hated them because they do not belong to the world, just as I do not belong to the world.* [15]*I am not asking you to take them out of the world, but I ask you to protect them from the evil one.* [16]*They do not belong to the world, just as I do not belong to the world.* [17]*Sanctify them in the truth; your word is truth.* [18]*As you have sent me into the world, so I have sent them into the world.* [19]*And for their sakes I sanctify myself, so that they also may be sanctified in truth.*

[20]*I ask not only on behalf of these, but also on behalf of those who will believe in me through their word,* [21]*that they may all be one. As you, Father, are in me and I am in you, may they also be in us, so that the world may believe that you have sent me.* [22]*The glory that you have given me I have given them, so that they may be one, as we are one,* [23]*I in them and you in me, that they may become completely one, so that the world may know that you have sent me and have*

loved them even as you have loved me. [24]*Father, I desire that those also, whom you have given me, may be with me where I am, to see my glory, which you have given me because you loved me before the foundation of the world.*

[25]*Righteous Father, the world does not know you, but I know you; and these know that you have sent me.* [26]*I made your name known to them, and I will make it known, so that the love with which you have loved me may be in them, and I in them.*

The final words of Jesus turn from an address to his disciples (John 14–16) to a prayer to his heavenly Father (John 17). Jesus prays not only for the disciples gathered around him at table, but also for all future disciples who will believe in Jesus through their word (verse 20). He prays that all believers may experience the gift of intimate union with the Father, in Jesus, through the transforming presence of the Holy Spirit. He then prays that, once disciples have experienced the loving unity between the Father and the Son, they might draw other believers into the unity of love that constitutes the heart of the Trinity.

Jesus addresses the Father as "Holy" (verse 11), and he prays that God will "sanctify" the disciples, making them holy as Jesus is holy (verses 17, 19). Sanctification is the interior work of the Holy Spirit, transforming believers within their deepest being into the image of Christ. Throughout his life, culminating in his death and resurrection, Jesus sanctified himself in his humanity for our sake. We are made holy through the working of the Holy Spirit given to us in the dying and rising of Christ. By uniting us intimately to Christ, the Spirit is the agent of our sanctification.

In his prayer for unity, Jesus wants to see the community of disciples united in the same kind of relationship that unites the inner life of God. The same love that unites the Father and the Son also unites believers among themselves and brings them into the inner dynamism of the divine life. Jesus' prayer "that they may all be one" is based on the reciprocal indwelling of the Father and the Son: "As you, Father, are in me and I am in you, may they also be in us" (verse 21). Unity is a characteristic of God and a gift of God; no genuine unity is possible apart from God. When this unity of mutual love is expressed among disciples, the church becomes a sacramental expression of the relational life of the Father, Son, and Holy Spirit.

As Jesus prays, his mission in the world is coming to an end, but that of the disciples is about to begin (verse 18). As Jesus revealed the Father throughout his life, so the mission of the disciples is to make God known to the world. The love within the Trinity becomes visible in the concreteness of mutual love among disciples "so that the world may believe" (verses 21, 23). The exterior mission to the world is based on the interior sanctification and unity of disciples. In their mutual love, disciples make visible to others the divine reality in which they live, and they reveal to the world the love of God for humanity. Dwelling in loving unity with God is indispensable for fruitful mission. By being one in love, the church spreads beyond itself the mystery of the Father, Son, and Holy Spirit that dwells within it.

Reflection and discussion

• What does it mean to me to be "holy"? What is the source of my sanctification?

• Why does Jesus pray "that they all may be one" (verse 21)? In what way is the unity of believers a witness to the world?

Prayer

Come, Holy Spirit, make your church holy and unite all disciples in the love which joins Jesus to the Father. May my love for others be a witness in the world, so that many may believe in Jesus whom the Father has loved before the foundation of the world.

He breathed on them and said to them, "Receive the Holy Spirit."
John 20:22

The Risen Lord Delivers His Spirit

JOHN 19:28–30 ²⁸*After this, when Jesus knew that all was now finished, he said (in order to fulfill the Scripture), "I am thirsty." ²⁹A jar full of sour wine was standing there. So they put a sponge full of the wine on a branch of hyssop and held it to his mouth. ³⁰When Jesus had received the wine, he said, "It is finished." Then he bowed his head and gave up his spirit.*

JOHN 20:19–23 ⁹*When it was evening on that day, the first day of the week, and the doors of the house where the disciples had met were locked for fear of the Jews, Jesus came and stood among them and said, "Peace be with you." ²⁰After he said this, he showed them his hands and his side. Then the disciples rejoiced when they saw the Lord. ²¹Jesus said to them again, "Peace be with you. As the Father has sent me, so I send you." ²²When he had said this, he breathed on them and said to them, "Receive the Holy Spirit. ²³If you forgive the sins of any, they are forgiven them; if you retain the sins of any, they are retained."*

At the completion of his life, as Jesus dies on the cross as the ultimate act of self-giving love, he announces "It is finished" (19:30). This exclamation is a shout of achievement, a triumphal announcement that his mission was accomplished. Having finished the work the Father had given him to do, his divine charge was now consummately concluded.

The narrator confirms this conclusion by commenting, "Then he bowed his head and gave up his spirit." On one level, this statement is simply an announcement that Jesus has exhaled his last breath. But as a declaration of his death's significance, the text announces that Jesus "handed over the Spirit." Bringing his divine mission to perfection means entrusting the Holy Spirit to the disciples at the foot of the cross. This is the new community that would be enlivened and empowered by the Spirit for mission.

At the appearance of the risen Jesus, the mandate Jesus gives his disciples is a summary of his own life and the life of the church: "As the Father has sent me, so I send you" (20:21). Jesus has revealed the Father for all to see— through his teachings, his healing signs, and finally through his total sacrifice on the cross. Now Jesus sends his disciples on that same mission. We are to be for the world what Jesus has been for the world. We are to embody the Father's love, to teach and heal, to comfort and bring peace, to love as Jesus loved.

Jesus enlivened and empowered his disciples as he breathed on them and said, "Receive the Holy Spirit" (20:22). As the Creator breathed life into the first human being (Gen 2:7), Jesus breathed his Spirit into God's new creation, the community of disciples sent out to forgive, heal, teach, and love. The Spirit is the ongoing presence of Christ, continuing Christ's mission in the world in every age.

By narrating the sending of the Holy Spirit, both at the death of Jesus on the cross and in his risen appearance, John's gospel connects the Spirit with the total act of Jesus' paschal mystery. Both in his death and his resurrection, Jesus poured forth his Spirit into the world. In this gospel, the church began as Jesus died on the cross, lifted up from the earth in glorious love and completing his great charge given him by the Father. But the church is commissioned and sent out by the risen Christ, gloriously present to his disciples and breathing his life into their own. To this newborn and newly commissioned church, the glorious Christ gives over his Spirit.

Reflection and discussion

• How does John's gospel indicate that the Holy Spirit is sent forth from the total gift of Christ's death and resurrection?

• What are the major differences in the way that Luke and John present the coming of the Holy Spirit to the church?

• What help from the Holy Spirit do I need to continue the mission of Jesus this day? What specific task has the Spirit given me today?

Prayer

Come, Holy Spirit. As you were delivered over by the crucified and risen Lord, you have been sent to Christian disciples to continue the saving work of Jesus in the world. Strengthen me to teach, heal, forgive, and love in his name.

SUGGESTIONS FOR FACILITATORS, GROUP SESSION 4

1. Welcome group members and ask if anyone has any questions, announcements, or requests.

2. You may want to pray this prayer as a group:

Loving Father, you have renewed creation through the sending of your Son into the world and through the gift of the Spirit of truth. As Jesus handed over his Spirit on the cross and breathed his Spirit into the world, he assured us that he would remain with us always. May rivers of living water fill our hearts and make us holy people. Baptize us in your Holy Spirit and give us new birth from above. May we respond to the gusting movements of the Spirit and be united in the love of Christ so that the world may believe.

3. Ask one or both of the following questions:
   - What is the most difficult part of this study for you?
   - What insights stand out to you from the lessons this week?

4. Discuss lessons 13 through 18. Choose one or more of the questions for reflection and discussion from each lesson to discuss as a group. You may want to ask group members which question was most challenging or helpful to them as you review each lesson.

5. Keep the discussion moving, but allow time for the questions that provoke the most discussion. Encourage the group members to use "I" language in their responses.

6. After talking over each lesson, instruct group members to complete lessons 19 through 24 on their own during the six days before the next group meeting. They should write out their own answers to the questions as preparation for next week's session.

7. Ask the group what encouragement they need for the coming week. Ask the members to pray for the needs of one another during the week.

8. Conclude by praying aloud together the prayer at the end of one of the lessons discussed. You may choose to conclude the prayer by asking members to pray aloud any requests they may have.

If the Spirit of him who raised Jesus from the dead dwells in you,
he who raised Christ from the dead will give life to your mortal bodies
also through his Spirit that dwells in you. Rom 8:11

The Spirit of God Dwells in You

ROMANS 8:1–17 *¹There is therefore now no condemnation for those who are in Christ Jesus. ²For the law of the Spirit of life in Christ Jesus has set you free from the law of sin and of death. ³For God has done what the law, weakened by the flesh, could not do: by sending his own Son in the likeness of sinful flesh, and to deal with sin, he condemned sin in the flesh, ⁴so that the just requirement of the law might be fulfilled in us, who walk not according to the flesh but according to the Spirit. ⁵For those who live according to the flesh set their minds on the things of the flesh, but those who live according to the Spirit set their minds on the things of the Spirit. ⁶To set the mind on the flesh is death, but to set the mind on the Spirit is life and peace. ⁷For this reason the mind that is set on the flesh is hostile to God; it does not submit to God's law—indeed it cannot, ⁸and those who are in the flesh cannot please God.*

⁹But you are not in the flesh; you are in the Spirit, since the Spirit of God dwells in you. Anyone who does not have the Spirit of Christ does not belong to him. ¹⁰But if Christ is in you, though the body is dead because of sin, the Spirit is life because of righteousness. ¹¹If the Spirit of him who raised Jesus from the dead dwells in you, he who raised Christ from the dead will give life to your mortal bodies also through his Spirit that dwells in you.

[12]So then, brothers and sisters, we are debtors, not to the flesh, to live according to the flesh—[13]for if you live according to the flesh, you will die; but if by the Spirit you put to death the deeds of the body, you will live. [14]For all who are led by the Spirit of God are children of God. [15]For you did not receive a spirit of slavery to fall back into fear, but you have received a spirit of adoption. When we cry, "Abba! Father!" [16]it is that very Spirit bearing witness with our spirit that we are children of God, [17]and if children, then heirs, heirs of God and joint heirs with Christ—if, in fact, we suffer with him so that we may also be glorified with him.

P aul proclaims victory "to those who are in Christ Jesus" (verse 1) over the tyranny of sin, death, and law. This liberating triumph is a result of Christ's dying and rising and its power is integrated into the internal lives of believers by the Holy Spirit. When God sends his Spirit into the hearts of believers, they are freed for praise, witness, and service, to live "according to the Spirit" (verse 4).

Paul contrasts two opposite ways of life: life in the flesh, a way that is closed and hostile to God; and life in the Spirit, a way that is open and responsive to God (verses 5–6, 12–13). The mindset of a person living in the flesh is motivated by self-centered interests and is oriented toward death. The mindset of one living in the Spirit is empowered by God's liberating grace and is oriented toward life and peace (verses 5–6). The Holy Spirit actually dwells within the baptized Christian, transforming and vitalizing the person from the deepest insides. The Christian life is not just an agreement with the teachings of Jesus or an external identification with his cause; rather, it is an internal makeover in which the individual personally participates in divine life.

This indwelling, transforming power is alternately called "the Spirit of God" and "the Spirit of Christ" (verse 9). The Christian life ultimately consists of allowing "the Spirit of him who raised Jesus from the dead" to live within us (verse 11). Because the same holy power that dwelt so completely in Jesus is now dwelling in us, God is able to completely reorient our lives. The vivifying energy of the Holy Spirit works within us not only in the present but continuously into the future, and ultimately will even transform our bodies, making them like the body of the risen Christ. The life we now share in the Spirit, though still influenced by sin and death, is the life that we will have in full at the final resurrection when God will renew the heavens and the earth.

Paul described our incorporation into divine life through images of a family. If we are led by God's Spirit, we become "children of God" and are able to call upon God as "Abba! Father!" (verse 15–16). Life under the domination of sin makes us worried, fearful slaves; life in the Spirit makes us trusting, confident children. With his Spirit within us, we share in all the privileges of Christ. We become God's adopted children and we become co-heirs with Christ of all the glory the Father has given the Son (verse 17).

Life in God's renewing Spirit is not just an individual affair. Through the Spirit, we become part of a new community in Christ, the family of God. This confers upon us certain privileges and responsibilities toward other members of the family. Attitudes that enhance or destroy family life also build up or tear down the church. As we say the family prayer that Jesus taught us, and call upon God as Our Father, we are grateful for the presence of the Spirit of Christ who orients us to a life of praise, witness, and service.

Reflection and discussion

• What are the indications that I am living "in the Spirit" rather than "in the flesh"?

We are oriented toward life and pea... mindset of person living in flesh are motivated by self interest and death

• In what way do I experience life in God's Spirit as a grace or gift of God?

Ones living in spirit is empowered by God's liberating grace we are focused on life, peace after life with God and helping our community

• In what way does the Holy Spirit transform the interior lives of believers? How does this transformation give me greater freedom?

Holy power that dwelt in Jesus. now dwells in us - God is able to reorient our lives - we become God's children we don't need to worry about daily problems because we can see the bigger picture of after life and are free to praise and be a witness to God + live a life of service

• In what way is life in God's Spirit both a present and a future reality? In what ways do I experience God's promises for the future breaking into my present life?

• What are the privileges and responsibilities of being children in the family of God?

We become part of the community of Christ - the family of God which is a priviledge - use must our actions must enhance that Family not destroy it. That means treating everyone fairly and acting

Prayer *as Jesus would*

Come, Holy Spirit, free my life from the tyranny of sin and death so that I will be free for a life of witness and service. Live within my heart to make me a child of God and enable me to confidently cry out to God, my Father.

God, who searches the heart, knows what is the mind of the Spirit,
because the Spirit intercedes for the saints according to the will of God.
Rom 8:27

We Have the First Fruits
of the Spirit

ROMANS 8:18–27 *18I consider that the sufferings of this present time are not worth comparing with the glory about to be revealed to us. 19For the creation waits with eager longing for the revealing of the children of God; 20for the creation was subjected to futility, not of its own will but by the will of the one who subjected it, in hope 21that the creation itself will be set free from its bondage to decay and will obtain the freedom of the glory of the children of God. 22We know that the whole creation has been groaning in labor pains until now; 23and not only the creation, but we ourselves, who have the first fruits of the Spirit, groan inwardly while we wait for adoption, the redemption of our bodies. 24For in hope we were saved. Now hope that is seen is not hope. For who hopes for what is seen? 25But if we hope for what we do not see, we wait for it with patience.*

26Likewise the Spirit helps us in our weakness; for we do not know how to pray as we ought, but that very Spirit intercedes with sighs too deep for words. 27And God, who searches the heart, knows what is the mind of the Spirit, because the Spirit intercedes for the saints according to the will of God.

Paul describes the Christian life as living in the Spirit. Our lives have been given new purpose and have been transformed from the inside through the Holy Spirit who lives within us. Already in our present lives, we are redeemed in Christ and are able to live with confidence and compassion as God's children. Yet, Paul's view of the Spirit-filled life is a realistic one. He does not pretend that those who have received God's Spirit will have trouble-free lives. Though we have received wonderful promises of the glory to come, we still experience weakness and affliction. Because we have been incorporated into Christ through his Spirit, we share in both the suffering and the glory of Christ.

Paul compares our present experience in the Spirit to the "first fruits" of a crop (verse 23). The first fruits in ancient Israel were the initial yield of a field, which were offered to God in sacrifice and served as a promise of the remainder of the harvest to come. We might say today that we have a "down payment" of the Spirit, a partial experience of God's life that assures us that the fullness will be revealed in the future. Though God's Spirit has already made us children of God, we will receive our full inheritance when the harvest of God's glory is revealed.

All of creation is longing for the glorious goal that it shares with humanity. Though the material world is now subject to corruption and decay, God has implanted within it the seed of hope, giving creation a natural urge and yearning for future glory (verses 19–21). Paul describes this longing of creation as "groaning in labor pains" (verse 22), waiting for the time of deliverance, like a mother in the pangs of birth yearning for the delivery of her child. That is why the suffering that we experience now is small in comparison to that future glory (verse 18).

Through the gift of hope, the Holy Spirit orients us toward the future, toward a final, radical act of God's Spirit still to come (verses 24–25). The Spirit is now the ground of our hope for living in the tension between suffering and glory. This hope is far more than a form of wishful thinking; it is a patient, yet confident waiting. Our hope is certain because we already have a foretaste of its fulfillment in our present experience of God's Spirit.

The Holy Spirit helps us in our weakness and intercedes for us in prayer (verses 26–27). Without the Spirit we are at a loss to know how to communicate with God. All we know how to do is "groan inwardly" (verse 23), but the Spirit intercedes for us and transforms our groaning into "sighs too deep for words," translating our words of prayer into the language of God's world. When we pray, "Abba, Father," God searches our hearts and hears his own Spirit praying within us. Through restoring our communication with God, the work of the Spirit is our foretaste of that transformed union with God for which we long.

Reflection and discussion

• In what way is my experience of the Holy Spirit like a crop's "first fruits" or like a down payment guaranteeing the balance?

We have received the gifts of the H.S. but we will have to wait for our final reward when God's glory is revealed to us

• What is the difference between "hope" and "wishful thinking"? What does it mean to "hope for what we do not see"?

When you wish you have no idea if it will come true, but when you hope you are confident of the outcome and just need to be patient.

• How does the Holy Spirit help me to pray? What evidence do I have that God's Spirit is praying within me?

Prayer

Come, Holy Spirit, help me in my weakness and my sufferings. You are God's promise of the complete redemption and salvation that awaits us. Pray within me with sighs too deep for words, so that I can express my prayers and hopes to my saving God.

We have received not the spirit of the world, but the Spirit that is from God, so that we may understand the gifts bestowed on us by God. 1 Cor 2:12

The Spirit Searches Even the Depths of God

1 CORINTHIANS 2:1–16 *¹When I came to you, brothers and sisters, I did not come proclaiming the mystery of God to you in lofty words or wisdom. ²For I decided to know nothing among you except Jesus Christ, and him crucified. ³And I came to you in weakness and in fear and in much trembling. ⁴My speech and my proclamation were not with plausible words of wisdom, but with a demonstration of the Spirit and of power, ⁵so that your faith might rest not on human wisdom but on the power of God.*

⁶Yet among the mature we do speak wisdom, though it is not a wisdom of this age or of the rulers of this age, who are doomed to perish. ⁷But we speak God's wisdom, secret and hidden, which God decreed before the ages for our glory. ⁸None of the rulers of this age understood this; for if they had, they would not have crucified the Lord of glory. ⁹But, as it is written,

"What no eye has seen, nor ear heard,
nor the human heart conceived,
what God has prepared for those who love him"—

¹⁰these things God has revealed to us through the Spirit; for the Spirit searches everything, even the depths of God. ¹¹For what human being knows what is truly human except the human spirit that is within? So also no one comprehends what is truly God's except the Spirit of God. [12]*Now we have received not the spirit of the world, but the Spirit that is from God, so that we may understand the gifts bestowed on us by God.* [13]*And we speak of these things in words not taught by human wisdom but taught by the Spirit, interpreting spiritual things to those who are spiritual.*

[14]*Those who are unspiritual do not receive the gifts of God's Spirit, for they are foolishness to them, and they are unable to understand them because they are discerned spiritually.* [15]*Those who are spiritual discern all things, and they are themselves subject to no one else's scrutiny.*

[16]*"For who has known the mind of the Lord*
so as to instruct him?"
But we have the mind of Christ.

Paul knew that the wisdom of God is summed up in the cross of Jesus Christ. This is a divine wisdom that cannot be understood through human reason, but can only be revealed to human beings through the Holy Spirit. This wisdom of God is beyond what the human mind can know and what the heart can imagine (verse 9). Only the Holy Spirit, who comprehends the depth of God, can enable us to understand the gifts that have been bestowed on us by God (verse 12).

Just as every human being has a depth that no one else can penetrate and understand, so there is a depth in God that is known only to God's Spirit (verse 11). Therefore, those who want to grasp what God has done in Christ and apprehend God's wisdom must be in touch with the Holy Spirit. Because God is so great and so totally holy, a connection with God's Spirit is the only way we can possibly conceive of what God has done for us through Christ crucified. Without the Spirit, we resist and reject God's wisdom as "foolishness" (verse 14). Only the Spirit enlightens us and transforms us so that "we have the mind of Christ" (verse 15).

Because Paul knew that he preached God's wisdom, "secret and hidden, which God decreed before the ages for our glory" (verse 7), he refused to use grandiose eloquence and rhetorical frills (verse 1). Paul wanted his preaching strategy to be consistent with the gospel he proclaimed, the message of Jesus Christ crucified. He knew that slick and superficial packaging was inappropriate and useless for proclaiming the mystery of a God who refused to play human games of power and prestige.

Instead, Paul came "in weakness and in fear and in much trembling" (verse 3), contrasting his own human frailty and God's strength. Because Paul presented the gospel in this way, his listeners could understand that their faith relied, not on human wisdom, but on the power of God's Spirit (verse 4–5). Those who follow the "wisdom of this age" (verse 6) remain unenlightened and spiritually immature, while those who attend to God's wisdom receive the gifts of God's Spirit.

Reflection and discussion

• What is the difference between human wisdom and the wisdom of God? How does Paul help his listeners and his readers to have "the mind of Christ"?

Human wisdom, at best, can only understand earthly matters. only the Holy Spirit. can comprehend what God has done in christ crucified - In order for humans to understand, God's wisdom, we must be in touch with the Holy spirit. Paul help understanding by not speaking in lofty words - but word, guide by the spirit

• What does Paul's evangelization strategy teach me about witnessing to the gospel of Christ's cross?

Prayer

Come, Holy Spirit. You lead me to an eternal wisdom, planned for my glory before the world began. Give me the mind of Christ so that I may be able to interpret spiritual things and discern all things. Enlighten my mind with understanding and enkindle my heart with love.

Now there are varieties of gifts, but the same Spirit;
and there are varieties of services, but the same Lord. 1 Cor 12:4–5

The Manifold Gifts
of the Spirit

1 CORINTHIANS 12:1–11 *¹Now concerning spiritual gifts, brothers and sisters, I do not want you to be uninformed. ²You know that when you were pagans, you were enticed and led astray to idols that could not speak. ³Therefore I want you to understand that no one speaking by the Spirit of God ever says "Let Jesus be cursed!" and no one can say "Jesus is Lord" except by the Holy Spirit.*

⁴Now there are varieties of gifts, but the same Spirit; ⁵and there are varieties of services, but the same Lord; ⁶and there are varieties of activities, but it is the same God who activates all of them in everyone. ⁷To each is given the manifestation of the Spirit for the common good. ⁸To one is given through the Spirit the utterance of wisdom, and to another the utterance of knowledge according to the same Spirit, ⁹to another faith by the same Spirit, to another gifts of healing by the one Spirit, ¹⁰to another the working of miracles, to another prophecy, to another the discernment of spirits, to another various kinds of tongues, to another the interpretation of tongues. ¹¹All these are activated by one and the same Spirit, who allots to each one individually just as the Spirit chooses.

The gifts that fill the church are described by Paul as charisms, that is, manifestations of God's grace. These gifts are freely given to individual believers and they are activated in each person by the Holy Spirit. Paul describes a church filled with charisms, in which all the members contribute their own unique gifts for building up the whole community. The power of God's Spirit is palpably present, working through the many complimentary gifts of each member of the community.

Paul offers nine examples of these gifts of the Spirit, expressing them as common occurrences in the church (verses 8–10). The list simply represents the diversity of the Spirit's manifestations and is not exhaustive, since other lists of gifts are found in other letters of Paul. The same community that prized the intellectual gift of uttering wisdom also valued the highly emotional gift of speaking in tongues. Healings, miracles, and prophetic speech seem to be regular events within the community. This rich diversity of spiritual gifts within the individual members of the church was activated by the same divine source, the Holy Spirit (verse 11).

Paul wanted the community to understand that merely expressing a sign of the spiritual world, like the ecstatic utterances of those who worship pagan idols, does not indicate a true gift from God's Spirit (verses 1–2). The first criterion of a genuine gift from the Holy Spirit is that the person confesses "Jesus is Lord" (verse 3). This acknowledgment of Jesus' lordship, lived authentically in a person's life, indicates that a person is living in the realm of the Spirit's power. The second criterion of an authentic gift is that it is exercised "for the common good" (verse 7). Gifts of the Spirit are not given for the personal glorification or status of the one receiving them. A genuine gift must be employed for the benefit of the whole community.

In three parallel statements, Paul states that there are varieties of gifts, but the same Spirit; varieties of services, but the same Lord; and varieties of activities, but the same God who activates all of them in everyone (verses 4–6). The rich diversity of the divine presence among believers—experienced as Spirit, Lord, and God—is the foundation for the abundant variety of gifts in the church. Great variety exists within the unity of the church because the source of the church's life is the one God manifested as three divine persons.

Reflection and discussion

• How are Paul's two criteria for discerning a true gift of the Holy Spirit still effective today?

The person must believe in Jesus as God - That can be seen in his daily actions - 2nd the gifts must not be used for personal gain or profit

• Why is both unity and diversity important for Christ's church?

• What gift, service, or activity do I have to offer to the church? How do I know whether or not it comes from the Holy Spirit?

The gift of time thru volunteering - only way I will quit because it was getting positive strokes - Emphasis on me not service

Prayer

Come, Holy Spirit, fill your church with gifts in abundance and unite believers as one body. Help me discern the gifts you have given me to serve others and teach me to proclaim with my life that Jesus is Lord.

For in the one Spirit we were all baptized into one body—Jews or Greeks, slaves or free—and we were all made to drink of one Spirit. 1 Cor 12:13

One Body United in One Spirit

1 CORINTHIANS 12:12–31 *¹²For just as the body is one and has many members, and all the members of the body, though many, are one body, so it is with Christ. ¹³For in the one Spirit we were all baptized into one body—Jews or Greeks, slaves or free—and we were all made to drink of one Spirit.*

¹⁴Indeed, the body does not consist of one member but of many. ¹⁵If the foot were to say, "Because I am not a hand, I do not belong to the body," that would not make it any less a part of the body. ¹⁶And if the ear were to say, "Because I am not an eye, I do not belong to the body," that would not make it any less a part of the body. ¹⁷If the whole body were an eye, where would the hearing be? If the whole body were hearing, where would the sense of smell be? ¹⁸But as it is, God arranged the members in the body, each one of them, as he chose. ¹⁹If all were a single member, where would the body be? ²⁰As it is, there are many members, yet one body. ²¹The eye cannot say to the hand, "I have no need of you," nor again the head to the feet, "I have no need of you." ²²On the contrary, the members of the body that seem to be weaker are indispensable, ²³and those members of the body that we think less honorable we clothe with greater honor, and our less respectable members are treated with greater respect; ²⁴whereas our more respectable members do not need this. But God has so arranged the body, giving the greater honor to the inferior member, ²⁵*that there may be no dissension within the body, but the members may have the same care for one another.* ²⁶*If one member suffers, all suffer together with it; if one member is honored, all rejoice together with it.*

²⁷*Now you are the body of Christ and individually members of it.* ²⁸*And God has appointed in the church first apostles, second prophets, third teachers; then deeds of power, then gifts of healing, forms of assistance, forms of leadership, various kinds of tongues.* ²⁹*Are all apostles? Are all prophets? Are all teachers? Do all work miracles?* ³⁰*Do all possess gifts of healing? Do all speak in tongues? Do all interpret?* ³¹*But strive for the greater gifts. And I will show you a still more excellent way.*

P aul describes the ideal unity of the church within its great diversity through the metaphor of the body. The body is essentially a unity, though it is made up of many diverse parts and functions. Paul uses this image to describe the multiplicity, interdependence, and importance of all the members of the church.

Yet, Paul does not only compare the body to the community, but essentially to Christ himself: "so it is with Christ" (verse 12). The great variety of believers is bound in a living unity with the risen Christ. In him, the great diversity of the community and its many gifts becomes purposeful and beneficial. This unity in the body of Christ is realized through the work of the Holy Spirit: "In the one Spirit we were all baptized into one body" (verse 13). Through the power of the Spirit, even extreme ethnic and social incompatibility—Jews or Greeks, slaves or free people—is superseded and overcome when believers are baptized into Christ.

Paul's elaboration of the body metaphor emphasizes the necessity of diversity in the church. The essence of the body is its differentiation into diverse and complementary parts. Without this separation, the body could not function. By imagining scenarios in which various body parts ridiculously secede from the body, Paul shows how each member is essential to the whole (verses 15–17). Because each part of the body has its own unique purpose in the functioning of the whole, no member of the church should ever think that his or her contribution is unimportant. In fact, this design is set within the divine plan: "God arranged the members in the body, each one of them, as he chose" (verse 18).

Because all the members of the body need one another, no one should look down upon another. On the contrary, "the members of the body that seem to be weaker are indispensable" (verse 22), and those who seem to be strong ignore them at their own peril. If there is dissension and division among the members, the whole body suffers. Paul imagines a unifying synergy within the church in which all members share the joys and sorrows of one another (verse 26).

Paul applies his image of the body to the variety of the Spirit's gifts within the body of Christ. He lists eight examples of various ministries and functions within the community (verse 28). Some of them are the same as his previous list of gifts (12:8–10); others are different. His rhetorical questions emphasize that everyone cannot have the same gift and no one can have all the gifts (verses 29–30). Paul urges the church to strive for unity, not uniformity. This is only possible when the diversity of the Spirit's gifts is honored, and the Spirit is allowed to activate the various manifestations of God's grace within the living body of Christ.

Reflection and discussion

• What are the primary barriers to the proper functioning of the church as the body of Christ, according to Paul's teaching?

which individual parts do not function together - one part may look down on another or feel it is more impt.

• In what way does Paul encourage unity rather than uniformity within the church? What is the difference?

The diversity of the gifts of the H.S. are honored and respected - All members share the joys and sorrows of others - which unites them - we do not want a uniform church where all member has the same roles and jobs. This does not allow for diversity

• How is the truth of verse 26 illustrated in my own physical body? in my church?

• How could my local church become more fully the body of Christ?

• How does Paul's teaching challenge my understanding of the workings of the Holy Spirit within Christ's church? What point do I want to remember most?

Prayer

Come, Holy Spirit, empower the members of the church to function together as the body of Christ in the world. Break down the divisions that divide God's people and unite them with a deep desire to serve one another in love.

Now the Lord is the Spirit, and where the Spirit of the Lord is,
there is freedom. 2 Cor 3:17

The Ministry of the Spirit Comes in Glory

2 CORINTHIANS 3:1–18 *¹Are we beginning to commend ourselves again? Surely we do not need, as some do, letters of recommendation to you or from you, do we? ²You yourselves are our letter, written on our hearts, to be known and read by all; ³and you show that you are a letter of Christ, prepared by us, written not with ink but with the Spirit of the living God, not on tablets of stone but on tablets of human hearts.*

⁴Such is the confidence that we have through Christ toward God. ⁵Not that we are competent of ourselves to claim anything as coming from us; our competence is from God, ⁶who has made us competent to be ministers of a new covenant, not of letter but of spirit; for the letter kills, but the Spirit gives life.

⁷Now if the ministry of death, chiseled in letters on stone tablets, came in glory so that the people of Israel could not gaze at Moses' face because of the glory of his face, a glory now set aside, ⁸how much more will the ministry of the Spirit come in glory? ⁹For if there was glory in the ministry of condemnation, much more does the ministry of justification abound in glory! ¹⁰Indeed, what once had glory has lost its glory because of the greater glory; ¹¹for if what was set aside came through glory, much more has the permanent come in glory!

¹²*Since, then, we have such a hope, we act with great boldness,* ¹³*not like Moses, who put a veil over his face to keep the people of Israel from gazing at the end of the glory that was being set aside.* ¹⁴*But their minds were hardened. Indeed, to this very day, when they hear the reading of the old covenant, that same veil is still there, since only in Christ is it set aside.* ¹⁵*Indeed, to this very day whenever Moses is read, a veil lies over their minds;* ¹⁶*but when one turns to the Lord, the veil is removed.* ¹⁷*Now the Lord is the Spirit, and where the Spirit of the Lord is, there is freedom.* ¹⁸*And all of us, with unveiled faces, seeing the glory of the Lord as though reflected in a mirror, are being transformed into the same image from one degree of glory to another; for this comes from the Lord, the Spirit.*

P aul uses another metaphor for the Christian community: "a letter of Christ" (verse 3). The community is a letter "written not with ink but with the Spirit of the living God," a letter written "not on tablets of stone but on tablets of human hearts." This is a letter that can be read and understood by everyone (verse 2), because whenever anyone sees the life of the community, they will know that the church has received the gift of the Holy Spirit as a result of the ministry of Paul among them. In this way, the community can be seen as "a letter of recommendation" for Paul, as a testament to his authenticity as an apostle of Christ.

Paul and the Christian community are ministers of the "new covenant" (verse 6), a covenant in which God's law is written not on stone, but on the hearts of God's people. Through the covenant inaugurated by Christ, God has responded to the promises he gave through Ezekiel: "I will put my spirit within you" (Ezek 36:27). The promised restoration is taking place as the new covenant is ministered in the church; God is breathing his Spirit on the dry bones of his people (Ezek 37:9–10). Paul underlines the work of Christ as a covenant "not of letter but of spirit." The "letter" is the written expression of God's will without the empowering work of the Holy Spirit, but the Spirit writes God's will on human hearts. The covenant with Moses had resulted in dried up bones, and the tablets of stone had no power to restore the people of God. But the new covenant would enliven God's people because "the Spirit gives life" (verse 6).

Paul compares Moses' ministry of the written law to his own life-giving "ministry of the Spirit" (verse 8). Though God's covenant on Mount Sinai came in glory and shone on the face of Moses (Exod 34:29–35), the glory of the new covenant shines far brighter with more permanent splendor (verses 9–11). The veil that covered the face of Moses and the minds of those who heard "the reading of the old covenant" has been removed from those who turn to the Lord in his Spirit (verses 13–16).

The essential work of the Holy Spirit is to reproduce the image of God again in the people of God. That divine image is replicated perfectly in Christ, so the Spirit is given to transform us into the likeness of Christ. Through the Holy Spirit, we experience the glory of Christ "with unveiled faces," and we see that glory "as though reflected in a mirror" (verse 18). Gradually, then, we are transformed into the image of God, the likeness of Christ—a process that can only come through the work of the Holy Spirit in the new covenant. This transformation that has already begun in us through the Spirit—"from one degree of glory to another"—will be perfected in the glorious resurrection to come.

Reflection and discussion

• What is the difference between following God's will with "the letter" and with "the Spirit" (verse 6)? Why does only the Spirit give me life?

The letter of the law is following rules and regulations the Do's, and Don't - The Spirit of the law is having the Divine Christ living within us and behaving in the Spirit christ only the Spirit can transform us into the likeness of christ

• In what experiences do I see the glory of Christ with an unveiled face? What can cause my vision of Christ to become veiled?

• The work of the Holy Spirit reproduces the image of God in the people of God by transforming us into the likeness of Christ. How do I open my life to this transforming process?

• Why will our transformation in the Spirit be complete only at our future resurrection?

Because that is when God's glory will be revealed

• Paul says that the Spirit of the Lord gives us new hope, new boldness, and new freedom. What changes do I notice as I open my life to God's Spirit?

calmer - less jealous less competitive

Prayer

Come, Holy Spirit, help me look for the manifestations of God's glory in the beauty of creation and the splendor of the sacraments. Work gradually but steadily within me to transform me into the likeness of Christ.

SUGGESTIONS FOR FACILITATORS, GROUP SESSION 5

1. Welcome group members and ask if anyone has any questions, announcements, or requests.

2. You may want to pray this prayer as a group:
Abba, Father, you have sent the Spirit of your Son into our hearts to assure us that we are your adopted children and members of your family. Give us hope for the future you have planned for us, and assure us that we will inherit all the blessings and glory you have given to Christ, your Son. Teach us to pray as your Spirit prays within us, and give us gifts from your Spirit to use for the service of Christ's church. Unite all your people as one body in Christ so that we can proclaim to the world that Jesus is Lord.

3. Ask one or both of the following questions:
   • What most intrigued you from this week's study?
   • What makes you want to know and understand more of God's word?

4. Discuss lessons 19 through 24. Choose one or more of the questions for reflection and discussion from each lesson to talk over as a group.

5. Ask the group members to name one thing they have most appreciated about the way the group has worked during this Bible study. Ask group members to discuss any changes they might suggest in the way the group works in future studies.

6. Invite group members to complete lessons 25 through 30 on their own during the six days before the next meeting. They should write out their own answers to the questions as preparation for next week's session.

7. Ask group members to take notice of how many times the Holy Spirit is mentioned in the liturgy of the church on Sunday, and invite them to reflect on the Spirit's role in the Eucharist.

8. Conclude by praying aloud together the prayer at the end of one of the lessons discussed. You may want to conclude the prayer by asking members to voice prayers of thanksgiving.

God has sent the Spirit of his Son into our hearts, crying, "Abba! Father!"
So you are no longer a slave but a child,
and if a child then also an heir, through God. Gal 4:6–7

Adopted Children of the Father

GALATIANS 3:27—4:7 *²⁷As many of you as were baptized into Christ have clothed yourselves with Christ. ²⁸There is no longer Jew or Greek, there is no longer slave or free, there is no longer male and female; for all of you are one in Christ Jesus. ²⁹And if you belong to Christ, then you are Abraham's offspring, heirs according to the promise.*

4 ¹My point is this: heirs, as long as they are minors, are no better than slaves, though they are the owners of all the property; ²but they remain under guardians and trustees until the date set by the father. ³So with us; while we were minors, we were enslaved to the elemental spirits of the world. ⁴But when the fullness of time had come, God sent his Son, born of a woman, born under the law, ⁵in order to redeem those who were under the law, so that we might receive adoption as children. ⁶And because you are children, God has sent the Spirit of his Son into our hearts, crying, "Abba! Father!" ⁷So you are no longer a slave but a child, and if a child then also an heir, through God.

The Holy Spirit works within us at the deepest level. The "heart," in the language of the Bible, is the center of a person's inner life, the deepest source of a person's thoughts, feelings, and actions. As Paul explains, "God has sent the Spirit of his Son into our hearts" (4:6). Because the Spirit of Christ fills our hearts, a whole new way of life is possible: a life of genuine freedom, of joyful worship, and most of all, of family relationship with God.

With the Spirit of God's Son living in our hearts, we cry out "Abba! Father!" We truly share in the filial relationship of Jesus with God the Father. The early Christians preserved the Aramaic form of address to God, Abba, to emphasize the characteristic way that Jesus spoke to God during his historical life. Jesus taught his disciples to call upon God as "Father," but his Spirit in our hearts brings us directly into God's family, so that we truly are legitimate children of the Father.

If we "belong to Christ," we become "heirs" of all that God promised to his people, beginning with Abraham and his descendants (3:29). Before the coming of Christ, God's people were like "minors" who remained under the care of guardians "until the date set by the father" for them to inherit the estate (4:1–2). This condition of being minors was no better than being slaves in the household, bound to the uncontrollable forces of the world (4:3). But when God sent his Son, in "the fullness of time," God ended this period of enslavement and the age of minority (4:4–5). We were redeemed from slavery and adopted by God as children like his Son, partaking of the heritage of the Father's estate.

The work of God's Spirit in Christian baptism incorporates us "into Christ" (3:27). Like the newly baptized who put on white garments, the Christian is "clothed" with Christ. This new identity in the family of God breaks down boundaries and distinctions that formerly separated people from one another. To identify oneself or others primarily according to ethnic, social, or gender categories is no longer appropriate for those who have been baptized into Christ. Through the Holy Spirit's work in baptism, a new creation occurs, in which "there is no longer Jew or Greek, there is no longer slave or free, there is no longer male and female" (3:28).

Throughout his ministry, Paul demonstrated the practical relevance of this liturgical expression of baptism's meaning: "You are all one in Christ Jesus." This unity does not mean that ethnic, social, and sexual differences between people disappear. Rather, unity in Christ destroys divisions, stratification, and hostility between people. In the family of God, these differences become irrelevant. Paul showed Jewish Christians how to eat and socialize with Greek Gentiles. He showed Christian slave owners how to look upon their servants as brothers and sisters in Christ. He worked side by side with women and related to them as partners in his ministry. Truly, the Holy Spirit who fills the heart of a baptized Christian gives new vision and new orientation to the one who is clothed with Christ.

Reflection and discussion

• How does the Father adopt me into his own family? What are the consequences for my future?

During baptism thru the spirit we become children of God and we become heirs to all that God promised

• How does it feel emotionally to be able to cry out in the Spirit, "Abba! Father!"?

• What are the practical consequences of the baptismal statement, "You are all one in Christ Jesus," for the world in which I live?

Differences become irrelevant We treat everyone as family

Prayer

Come, Holy Spirit, live deep within my heart, filling me with the joy and confidence of being a child of the Father. Break down the ethnic, social, and sexual barriers that separate people, and unite them in the new creation of Christian baptism.

The fruit of the Spirit is love, joy, peace, patience, kindness, generosity, faithfulness, gentleness, and self-control. Gal 5:22

The Fruit of the Holy Spirit

GALATIANS 5:13–26 *¹³For you were called to freedom, brothers and sisters; only do not use your freedom as an opportunity for self-indulgence, but through love become slaves to one another. ¹⁴For the whole law is summed up in a single commandment, "You shall love your neighbor as yourself." ¹⁵If, however, you bite and devour one another, take care that you are not consumed by one another.*

¹⁶Live by the Spirit, I say, and do not gratify the desires of the flesh. ¹⁷For what the flesh desires is opposed to the Spirit, and what the Spirit desires is opposed to the flesh; for these are opposed to each other, to prevent you from doing what you want. ¹⁸But if you are led by the Spirit, you are not subject to the law. ¹⁹Now the works of the flesh are obvious: fornication, impurity, licentiousness, ²⁰idolatry, sorcery, enmities, strife, jealousy, anger, quarrels, dissensions, factions, ²¹envy, drunkenness, carousing, and things like these. I am warning you, as I warned you before: those who do such things will not inherit the kingdom of God.

²²By contrast, the fruit of the Spirit is love, joy, peace, patience, kindness, generosity, faithfulness, ²³gentleness, and self-control. There is no law against such things. ²⁴And those who belong to Christ Jesus have crucified the flesh with its passions and desires. ²⁵If we live by the Spirit, let us also be guided by the Spirit. ²⁶Let us not become conceited, competing against one another, envying one another.

One of the principle characteristics of life in God's Spirit is freedom. This freedom in the Spirit is a gift that increases in value as it is used and can be lost through misuse. It is not the freedom of permissive self-indulgence, which paradoxically is a kind of slavery. Genuine freedom is the opportunity to lovingly serve others. As Paul charges his listeners, "Through love become slaves to one another" (verse 13).

The sum and substance of Christian ethics is found in the single command: "You shall love your neighbor as yourself." Originated in the Torah (Lev 19:18) and taught by Jesus (Matt 22:39), the command to love is rooted in the love God has for us and the example of Jesus' love unto death. Those who have been set free by Jesus are given the vocation to love one another. This concrete self-giving to individual men and women is the essence of life in the Spirit.

Paul urges his hearers to "live by the Spirit," in contrast to gratifying "the desires of the flesh" (verse 16). Living in the Spirit suggests a daily, progressive opening of one's life to the expansive love experienced in Christ. This way of life is contrasted to the way of the flesh. "The flesh" does not refer to physical desires, human feelings, or sensual pleasures, all of which are part of the bodily reality of God's good creation. Rather, the flesh is those tendencies within human beings that are opposed to the Spirit, that is, our desire to turn in on ourselves and away from God. These two desires within a person's life, the Spirit and the flesh, are opposed to each other and battle over a person's freedom, which is assured by the Spirit and thwarted by the flesh.

The "works of the flesh" (verse 19–21) are all those actions that arise from a life opposed to the Spirit. Though they arise from within, they manifest themselves in a life that protects the self and dominates others. The "fruit of the Spirit" (verses 22–23), in contrast, is the result of a life rooted in Christ. Most of these virtues are described in other parts of Paul's letters as characteristics of God or Christ, so manifesting the Spirit's fruit is another aspect of clothing oneself in Christ. Unlike the gifts of the Spirit, which differ from person to person as the Spirit distributes them, the fruit of the Spirit is the same for everyone, the result of the cooperation between freedom and grace. The Spirit's fruit is produced when the garden sown in human freedom receives the life-giving rain of the Holy Spirit.

The list of the Spirit's fruit can often be helpful in distinguishing genuine guidance of the Holy Spirit from one's own subjective feelings and impulses. Though there is no fool-proof method of discerning the Spirit's work, we can follow the Spirit's trail by looking for the fruit. If one's choice or action is led by the Spirit, it will produce results like love, joy, peace, generosity, and faithfulness. If it results in hostility, jealousy, anger, hatred, or dissension, there is a good chance that the Spirit has nothing to do with it.

Reflection and discussion

• Why is life in God's Spirit a life of genuine freedom? How could I lose my freedom?

Genuine freedom is the opportunity to willingly / lovingly serve us. We can lose it by giving into desires of the flesh envy anger jealousy

• Why does Paul describe the results of life in the Spirit as "fruit"? How do I grow spiritual fruit?

Because everyone can bear them - when freedom & grace work together

• Which fruit of the Spirit is just beginning to bud in me? Which fruit is blossoming? Which is ripe for the harvest?

Prayer

Come, Holy Spirit, produce in me the character traits of Jesus Christ. Set me free to serve the needs of others. May your presence shine through me in love and joy, peace and patience, generosity and faithfulness.

I pray that, according to the riches of his glory, he may grant that
you may be strengthened in your inner being with power through his Spirit,
and that Christ may dwell in your hearts through faith,
as you are being rooted and grounded in love. Eph 3:16–17

God's Mystery Revealed by the Spirit

EPHESIANS 3:1–21 *¹This is the reason that I Paul am a prisoner for Christ Jesus for the sake of you Gentiles—²for surely you have already heard of the commission of God's grace that was given to me for you, ³and how the mystery was made known to me by revelation, as I wrote above in a few words, ⁴a reading of which will enable you to perceive my understanding of the mystery of Christ. ⁵In former generations this mystery was not made known to humankind, as it has now been revealed to his holy apostles and prophets by the Spirit: ⁶that is, the Gentiles have become fellow-heirs, members of the same body, and sharers in the promise in Christ Jesus through the gospel.*

⁷Of this gospel I have become a servant according to the gift of God's grace that was given to me by the working of his power. ⁸Although I am the very least of all the saints, this grace was given to me to bring to the Gentiles the news of the boundless riches of Christ, ⁹and to make everyone see what is the plan of the mystery hidden for ages in God who created all things; ¹⁰so that through the church the wisdom of God in its rich variety might now be made known to the rulers and authorities in the heavenly places. ¹¹This was in accordance with the eternal pur-

pose that he has carried out in Christ Jesus our Lord, [12]in whom we have access to God in boldness and confidence through faith in him. [13]I pray therefore that you may not lose heart over my sufferings for you; they are your glory.

[14]For this reason I bow my knees before the Father, [15]from whom every family in heaven and on earth takes its name. [16]I pray that, according to the riches of his glory, he may grant that you may be strengthened in your inner being with power through his Spirit, [17]and that Christ may dwell in your hearts through faith, as you are being rooted and grounded in love. [18]I pray that you may have the power to comprehend, with all the saints, what is the breadth and length and height and depth, [19]and to know the love of Christ that surpasses knowledge, so that you may be filled with all the fullness of God.

[20]Now to him who by the power at work within us is able to accomplish abundantly far more than all we can ask or imagine, [21]to him be glory in the church and in Christ Jesus to all generations, for ever and ever. Amen.

Paul proclaims the universality of the Spirit's work by speaking of the "mystery" of God's unifying plan. The first critical step in God's cosmic goal is unity between Jews and Gentiles, the beginning of a broad unity that will include all of creation. The joining of Jews and Gentiles expresses the oneness of all humanity in Christ, a unity that will be followed by the renewal of all created reality. This universal work of the Holy Spirit will eventually bring all things to their perfection.

This divine master plan was "hidden for ages in God who created all things" (verse 9), but is now being revealed. God made known this mystery first to Paul (verse 3), then to God's "holy apostles and prophets" (verse 5), then to everyone (verse 9), and finally to the "rulers and authorities in the heavenly places" (verse10). Everyone on earth and in heaven has now come to know God's vision for the glorious and unified church, God's "eternal purpose that he has carried out in Christ Jesus our Lord" (verse 11).

Paul's prayer for his readers addresses God confidently, trusting that God will give out of "the riches of his glory" (verse 16). He prays that God will give us inner strength through the Holy Spirit and that Christ will dwell in our hearts (verse 17). Our inner being, that invisible part of us that includes our minds and hearts, is the place where the power of God's Spirit works and where the Spirit of Christ dwells. This abiding presence of Christ through the

Spirit is established through the openness created by our faith and roots our lives in love. The petitions conclude with Paul's request that his readers have the power to comprehend the magnitude of Christ's love that fills the universe. This perception of the cosmic proportions of divine love, given through the inner working of the Holy Spirit, leads us to a sharing in "the fullness of God" (verse 18–19).

Union with God is the ultimate goal of humanity. It is a goal that we experience already in union with Christ, but a goal that we do not yet possess. Our goal remains to be fulfilled as we receive the gifts God gives us through the Holy Spirit and grow in our capacity to receive them. Even Paul's confident requests to God fall short of what God is able to do. The one who is able to accomplish within us "far more than all we can ask or imagine" will continue to complete his vast and eternal plan (verses 20–21). This mystery of God's unifying plan will continue to unfold as the Spirit works in the church, which is Christ's body, to all generations.

Reflection and discussion

• What is "the mystery hidden for ages in God"? What does this mean to me?

oneness of all humanity in God starting with Jews and gentiles

• If God's ultimate goal is a gift of God's grace, what is my role in its accomplishment?

prayer and treating people as christ would

• If God wishes to break down divisions between people, what are some of the major issues today which God's people must address?

immigration

inequality

fractured families

• Which phrase of Paul's prayer expresses a deep longing within myself?

That christ may dwell in your hearts thru faith as you are being grounded and rooted in love

• What words would I use to express Paul's prayer?

May the Holy Spirit fill your soul heart with Chis christ's love so your soul heart feels the fulness of God

Prayer

Come, Holy Spirit, strengthen my inner being with your power and help me comprehend Christ's vast love. I know that you are able to accomplish within me far more than I can even ask or imagine. I praise you for ever and ever.

Speaking the truth in love, we must grow up in every way into him who is the head, into Christ. Eph 4:15

Building Up the Body of Christ

EPHESIANS 4:1–16 *¹I therefore, the prisoner in the Lord, beg you to lead a life worthy of the calling to which you have been called, ²with all humility and gentleness, with patience, bearing with one another in love, ³making every effort to maintain the unity of the Spirit in the bond of peace. ⁴There is one body and one Spirit, just as you were called to the one hope of your calling, ⁵one Lord, one faith, one baptism, ⁶one God and Father of all, who is above all and through all and in all.*

⁷But each of us was given grace according to the measure of Christ's gift. ⁸Therefore it is said,

"When he ascended on high he made captivity itself a captive;

he gave gifts to his people."

⁹(When it says, "He ascended," what does it mean but that he had also descended into the lower parts of the earth? ¹⁰He who descended is the same one who ascended far above all the heavens, so that he might fill all things.) ¹¹The gifts he gave were that some would be apostles, some prophets, some evangelists, some pastors and teachers, ¹²to equip the saints for the work of ministry, for building up the body of Christ, ¹³until all of us come to the unity of the faith and of the knowledge of the Son of God, to maturity, to the measure of the full stature of Christ. [14]*We must no longer be children, tossed to and fro and blown about by every wind of doctrine, by people's trickery, by their craftiness in deceitful scheming.* [15]*But speaking the truth in love, we must grow up in every way into him who is the head, into Christ,* [16]*from whom the whole body, joined and knitted together by every ligament with which it is equipped, as each part is working properly, promotes the body's growth in building itself up in love.*

Paul urges the members of the church to maintain unity—a oneness that has been effected by Christ's work of reconciliation and has been given by the Holy Spirit. This "unity of the Spirit" (verse 3) is a divine gift, but a gift that must be preserved and cultivated as Christians live, work, and worship together. It is lived through practicing the virtues that make possible the church's harmony: humility, gentleness, patience, love, and peace (verse 2)—many of the same qualities that Paul lists as fruit of the Spirit (Gal 5:22–23).

The unity of Christ's church is rooted in the oneness of God, the ultimate source of all unity. Paul describes the church as "one body" which is animated by "one Spirit" (verse 4). This unified church strives toward its "one hope," the inheritance promised by the church's "one Lord" (verse 5). The church is united in the "one faith," the gospel it professes, and "one baptism," through which each member is initiated into the life of Christ. This series of seven facets of the church's unity culminates in the origin of its unity, the "one God and Father of all" (verse 6).

The unity of the body, enlivened by the Spirit, is composed of diverse parts, all of which contribute to the body's unified functioning. When Christ ascended, the Spirit of Christ descended upon the church, making Christ accessible to all people everywhere at all times (verses 7–10). This gift of God's grace is apportioned to each person in the form of spiritual gifts. In this way, all the parts of the body work together to produce the unified growth of the church. Some are "apostles" and "prophets," those witnesses and proclaimers who formed the church's foundation; some are "evangelists, some pastors and teachers," those who preach the gospel, shepherd the congregations, and feed the flock after the example of Jesus (verse 11).

The purpose of these gifts of the Spirit is "for building up the body of Christ" (verse 12). Each of these roles of leadership is designed "to equip the saints for the work of ministry," so that all God's people might be prepared to serve and contribute to the process of the body's growth. The ultimate goal of this growth is the church's unity in faith and knowledge and the "maturity" of the body of Christ (verse 13). Because this goal is not accomplished, but an ideal to work toward, the church is often characterized by immaturity and instability (verse 14). In the midst of the church's divisions, rivalries, suspicions, and general immaturity, the way to "grow up" is by "speaking the truth in love" (verse 15). Holding to the truth in a spirit of love is the only route to a fully mature Christian unity. In this way, the entire body grows up into Christ who is the body's "head."

Christ is both the source and the goal of the church's growth. As the head of the body, Christ directs its growth as each part and ligament is joined to make the whole body work and grow in unity. Those given the spiritual gifts to be apostles, prophets, evangelists, pastors, and teachers are themselves part of the body, not separate from it or placed over it. Like all the parts of the body, they are under the control of the head. The church will grow only in a spirit of love, that virtue which disregards self-indulgence and self-promotion and which honors self-giving and the well-being of others.

Reflection and discussion

• In what way is the unity of the church both a gift of God's grace and a task for human effort?

God gave us gift of unity but we have to work together to keep it one and not divide over jeulousies

• What indicates that the Holy Spirit calls everyone to the work of ministry in the church? How are God's people equipped for ministry?

Each has different gifts pastors apostles teacher

• In what way does my unique ministry contribute to the growth and maturity of Christ's body?

• Why is "speaking the truth in love" so essential for the maturity and unity of Christ's church? In what way can I hold to the truth in a spirit of love?

Because it is the one way the church can mature to gether it disregards self indulgence & self promotion

• Is it possible to love without speaking the truth? What is truth without love?

Prayer

Come, Holy Spirit, raise up gifted leaders in your church who will equip the body of Christ with the gifts of ministry. May the church grow into the fullness of Christ and be united in the one God and Father of all, who is above all and through all and in all.

Be filled with the Spirit, as you sing psalms and hymns and spiritual songs among yourselves, singing and making melody to the Lord in your hearts.

Eph 5:18–19

Live as Children of Light

EPHESIANS 5:6–20 *⁶Let no one deceive you with empty words, for because of these things the wrath of God comes on those who are disobedient. ⁷Therefore do not be associated with them. ⁸For once you were darkness, but now in the Lord you are light. Live as children of light—⁹for the fruit of the light is found in all that is good and right and true. ¹⁰Try to find out what is pleasing to the Lord. ¹¹Take no part in the unfruitful works of darkness, but instead expose them. ¹²For it is shameful even to mention what such people do secretly; ¹³but everything exposed by the light becomes visible, ¹⁴for everything that becomes visible is light. Therefore it says,*

"Sleeper, awake!
   Rise from the dead,
and Christ will shine on you."

¹⁵Be careful then how you live, not as unwise people but as wise, ¹⁶making the most of the time, because the days are evil. ¹⁷So do not be foolish, but understand what the will of the Lord is. ¹⁸Do not get drunk with wine, for that is debauchery; but be filled with the Spirit, ¹⁹as you sing psalms and hymns and spiritual songs among yourselves, singing and making melody to the Lord in your hearts, ²⁰giving thanks to God the Father at all times and for everything in the name of our Lord Jesus Christ.

Christian baptism in water and the Holy Spirit is initiation into a life of radical conversion. As a person is created anew in Christ, there is an internal change that must be expressed in a new way of life. Paul expresses this change that occurs within the baptized Christian by quoting from an early hymn of the baptismal liturgy: "Sleeper, awake! Rise from the dead, and Christ will shine on you" (verse 14). Sleep, death, and darkness are striking expressions of the condition of a person apart from Christ. Baptism is the action of God's Spirit by which a person awakens from sleep, rises from the dead, and responds to the light of Christ. Perhaps the hymn was sung as the newly baptized rose from the water to new life.

Paul urges the baptized Christians to "live as children of light" (verse 8). Though they once lived as darkness, embodying the night of ignorance and sin, they now live as light in the Lord. As believers, they will produce the "fruit of the light," that which is "good and right and true" (verse 9). Because of their inner transformation, those baptized into Christ will have an internal capacity to discern what is God's will in the circumstances of life (verses 10, 17). Since all of life after baptism becomes a sacrificial gift to God, the Christian must always seek to find out what offering is most "pleasing to the Lord." In contrast, those who live as darkness produce "unfruitful works" (verse 11) but they can be converted to the light as the baptized believer shines upon them. The power of the light not only exposes evil, but then penetrates whatever and whoever it illumines (verse 13).

"Be filled with the Spirit," Paul exhorts his listeners (verse 18). Allowing the Holy Spirit to be fully active in our lives means living wisely (verse 15) and making the most of every opportunity (verse 16). Time is a precious commodity, and Paul urges us to be alert for occasions to invest our energies in worthwhile pursuits. The admonition not to get drunk on wine refers to the pagan cults in which alcohol produced frenzied religious behavior. Life in the Spirit is the better way that Christians experience spiritual elation.

This uplifted delight in the Spirit is experienced in Christian worship. Believers gather to praise God with singing and respond to God's goodness with jubilant thanksgiving (verses 19–20). Like all Christian worship, these prayers are addressed to God the Father, in the name of our Lord Jesus Christ, and in the Holy Spirit.

Reflection and discussion

• How is the inner transformation of baptism expressed in the thoughts, feelings, attitudes, and actions of a Christian?

you will be able to discern God's will in circumstance of life. They found seek out to find out what is most pleasing to God

• What motivates me to live a life that is filled with the Spirit? How am I making progress?

• What practical advice of Paul do I want to incorporate into my life today?

Be filled with the Holy Spirit Live our lives wisely

Prayer

Come, Holy Spirit, raise me from sleep with the shining light of Christ. Help me put away the unfruitful works of darkness and practice only what is good, right, and true. Fill me with your energy and joy so that I may always live in thanksgiving to God.

As God's chosen ones, holy and beloved, clothe yourselves with compassion, kindness, humility, meekness, and patience. Col 3:12

New Life in the Spirit

COLOSSIANS 3:1–17 *¹So if you have been raised with Christ, seek the things that are above, where Christ is, seated at the right hand of God. ²Set your minds on things that are above, not on things that are on earth, ³for you have died, and your life is hidden with Christ in God. ⁴When Christ who is your life is revealed, then you also will be revealed with him in glory.*

⁵Put to death, therefore, whatever in you is earthly: fornication, impurity, passion, evil desire, and greed (which is idolatry). ⁶On account of these the wrath of God is coming on those who are disobedient. ⁷These are the ways you also once followed, when you were living that life. ⁸But now you must get rid of all such things—anger, wrath, malice, slander, and abusive language from your mouth. ⁹Do not lie to one another, seeing that you have stripped off the old self with its practices ¹⁰and have clothed yourselves with the new self, which is being renewed in knowledge according to the image of its creator. ¹¹In that renewal there is no longer Greek and Jew, circumcised and uncircumcised, barbarian, Scythian, slave and free; but Christ is all and in all!

¹²As God's chosen ones, holy and beloved, clothe yourselves with compassion, kindness, humility, meekness, and patience. ¹³Bear with one another and, if any-one has a complaint against another, forgive each other; just as the Lord has forgiven you, so you also must forgive. ¹⁴Above all, clothe yourselves with love, which binds everything together in perfect harmony. ¹⁵And let the peace of Christ

*rule in your hearts, to which indeed you were called in the one body. And be
thankful.* [16]*Let the word of Christ dwell in you richly; teach and admonish one
another in all wisdom; and with gratitude in your hearts sing psalms, hymns, and
spiritual songs to God.* [17]*And whatever you do, in word or deed, do everything in
the name of the Lord Jesus, giving thanks to God the Father through him.*

As people who have been baptized into Christ, we are united with him
through the Holy Spirit in such a way that we share in his death,
burial, and resurrection. Entering the water of baptism we die,
returning to the chaos from which the world was created. Then, like a child
emerging from the womb and Christ emerging victorious from the tomb, we
rise as newly created persons (verse 1). Yet, this new life is now "hidden with
Christ in God," destined to be revealed fully in the glorious future for which
we hope (verse 3–4). The "hidden" quality of our present life in Christ suggests that the splendor of divine grace that fills our lives cannot be seen or
appreciated by the world. Our divine indwelling is even half-hidden from
ourselves because it is cloaked in mystery. When Christ is fully revealed in
glory to all creation, then our glorious life in Christ will also be fully revealed.

Our new identity in union with Christ is both a gift and a call. Through his
Spirit, we are raised in Christ, with Christ, by Christ, to be like Christ. Our
baptismal rebirth requires that we become in practice what we truly are
through the grace of the sacrament. This lifelong process means dying to all
within us that is selfish, debased, and sinful (verses 5, 8–9), and rising to a life
characterized by gratitude, generosity, and love (verses 10, 12, 14). In speaking
about this transformation, Paul uses the baptismal image of taking off and
discarding the old clothing and putting on new garments. In Christian baptism, this is expressed through the white robes, symbolizing resurrected and
newly-created life.

This "new self" is continually being renewed by the Spirit and made into
"the image of its creator" (verse 10). The religious, racial, social, and cultural
barriers that so often divide humanity no longer have any significance when
all are united and centered in the risen Christ (verse 11). The hallmark of
Christian community is genuine love, that virtue which completes all the others and establishes the harmony and peace which characterizes life in Christ
(verses 14–15).

When we allow "the word of Christ" to dwell with us through the sacred Scriptures, our lives will overflow with wise teaching and grateful singing (verse 16). Our communal worship of God will expand into our daily living, so that we will do everything "in the name of the Lord Jesus" (verse 17). All of life will become a thanksgiving sacrifice offered to God, through Jesus Christ, in the unity of the Holy Spirit.

Reflection and discussion

• In what way is the font of baptism like a womb and a tomb?

Because entering of the water to baptism we die and then emerge from the womb and Christ emerge victorious from the tomb

• In what way is my new life still "hidden with Christ in God" (verse 3)? How is it already "revealed with Christ in glory" (verse 4)?

• How can I best make the encouragement of verse 17 a practical reality in my life today?

treating people like Jesus would

Prayer

Come, Holy Spirit, empower me to offer all my words and deeds to God the Father in the name of the Lord Jesus. Through your power I have been created anew in Christ through the dying and rising of Christian baptism. Help me live each day as God's new creation.

SUGGESTIONS FOR FACILITATORS, GROUP SESSION 6

1. Welcome group members and make any final announcements or requests.

2. You may want to pray this prayer as a group:

Merciful God, you have poured divine love into our hearts through the Holy Spirit and made us your children. Help us live in the Spirit as children of light, and give us the grace to manifest the fruit of your Spirit each day. May we break down the barriers that divide us from one another and show forth the unity that is your plan for all creation. As we study the Scriptures, give us the grace to speak the truth in love and to do everything in the name of the Lord Jesus.

3. Ask one or both of the following questions:
   - How has this study of the Holy Spirit enriched your life?
   - In what way has this study challenged you the most?

4. Discuss lessons 25 through 30. Choose one or more of the questions for reflection and discussion from each lesson to discuss as a group.

5. Ask the group if they would like to study another in the Threshold Bible Study series. Discuss the topic and dates, and make a decision among those interested. Ask the group members to suggest people they would like to invite to participate in the next study series.

6. Ask the group to discuss the insights that stand out most from this study over the past six weeks.

7. Conclude by praying aloud the following prayer or another of your own choosing:

Holy Spirit of the living God, you inspired the writers of the Scriptures and you have guided our study during these weeks. Continue to deepen our love for the word of God in the holy Scriptures and draw us more deeply into the heart of Jesus. We thank you for the confident hope you have placed within us and the gifts which build up the church. Through this study, lead us to worship and witness more fully and fervently, and bless us now and always with the fire of your love.

Ordering Additional Studies

AVAILABLE TITLES IN THIS SERIES INCLUDE...

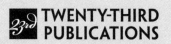

TO CHECK AVAILABILITY OR FOR A DESCRIPTION
OF EACH STUDY, VISIT OUR WEBSITE AT
www.ThresholdBibleStudy.com
OR CALL US AT **1-800-321-0411**